# Diagonal (or On-Point) Set

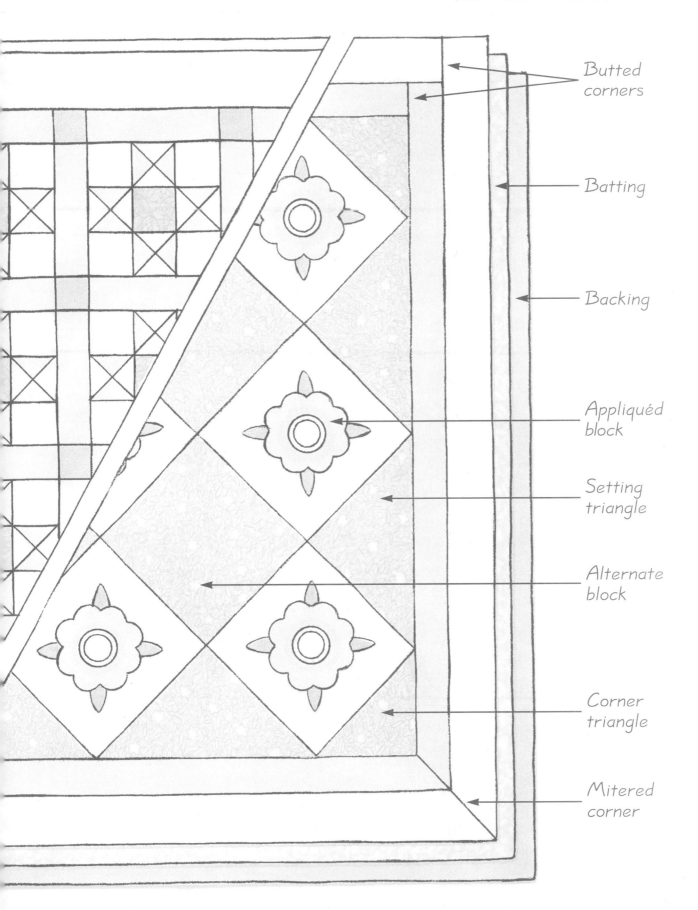

Butted corners

Batting

Backing

Appliquéd block

Setting triangle

Alternate block

Corner triangle

Mitered corner

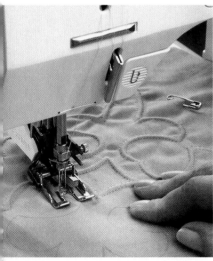

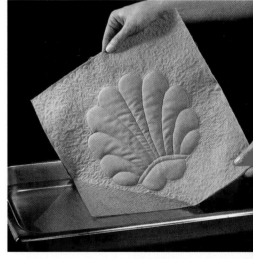

# Rodale's Successful Quilting Library™

# Fast & Fun Machine Quilting

*Karen Costello Soltys*
*Editor*

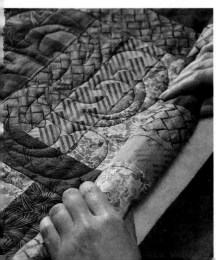

Rodale Press, Inc.
Emmaus, Pennsylvania

## OUR PURPOSE

*"We inspire and enable people to improve
their lives and the world around them."*

Editor: Karen Costello Soltys
Contributing Editors: Sarah Sacks Dunn and Jane Townswick
Writers: Laura Heine, Jeannette Muir, Susan Stein, Holice Turnbow, Debra Wagner, Hari Walner, Janet Wickell, and Julia Zgliniec
Designer: Sue Gettlin
Book Layout: Christopher Rhoads
Illustrators: Mario Ferro, Sandy Freeman, Sue Gettlin, John Kocon, and Christopher Rhoads
Photographer: Mitch Mandel
Photo Stylist: Stan Green
Model: Anne Cassar
Copy Editor: Erana Bumbardatore
Manufacturing Coordinator: Patrick Smith
Indexer: Nan Badgett

Editorial Assistance: Jodi L. Guiducci

*On the cover:* Somewhat Off Center by Laura Heine, Billings, Montana

**Rodale Home and Garden Books**
Vice President and Editorial Director: Margaret J. Lydic
Managing Editor, Quilt Books: Suzanne Nelson
Director of Design and Production: Michael Ward
Associate Art Director: Carol Angstadt
Studio Manager: Leslie Keefe
Copy Director: Dolores Plikaitis
Book Manufacturing Director: Helen Clogston

We're happy to hear from you.

For questions or comments concerning the editorial content of this book, please write to:

Rodale Press, Inc.
Book Readers' Service
33 East Minor Street
Emmaus, PA 18098

For more information about Rodale Press and the books and magazines we publish, visit our World Wide Web site at:
http://www.rodalepress.com

**Library of Congress Cataloging-in-Publication Data**

Rodale's successful quilting library.
    p.  cm.
  Includes index.
  ISBN 0–87596–761–2 (hc: v. 1:alk paper)
  1. Quilting. 2. Patchwork. I. Soltys, Karen Costello.  II. Rodale Press.
TT835.R622  1997
746.46'041—dc21          96–51316

Distributed in the book trade by St. Martin's Press

4 6 8 10 9 7 5 3  hardcover

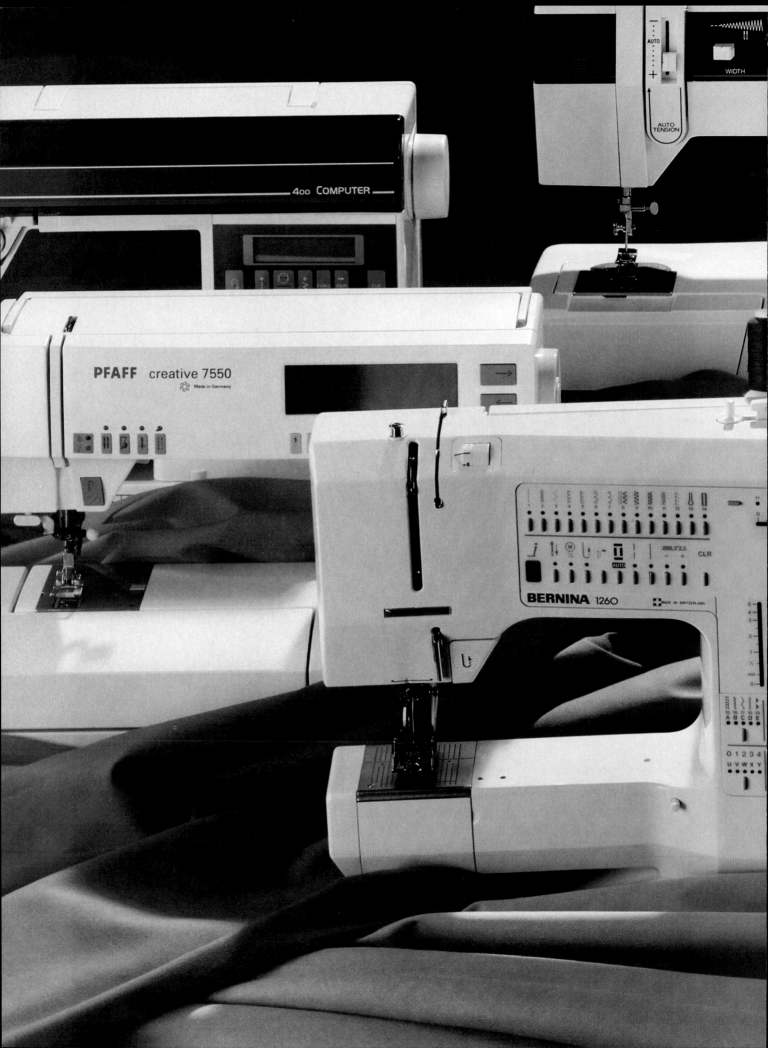

# Contents

# Introduction

**W**elcome to the world of *Fast and Fun Machine Quilting!* If you're like me, your interest in machine quilting started because you were looking for a way to turn your pieced or appliquéd quilt tops into actual, usable, *finished* quilts. I admit, I was tired of seeing a skinny stack of folded quilt tops in my sewing room that never managed to blossom into completed quilts, full of batting and defining stitches that could be displayed on beds, walls, or in the jelly cupboard in my living room.

I had heard that machine quilting was fast, so I purchased a walking foot, a spool of monofilament thread, and I was off—or so I thought. Let's just say that my first adventure in machine quilting was less than a success. Something was very wrong with my tension, the batting shifted all over the place, and I had pleats galore on the back of the quilt. It was not a pretty picture. But I was willing to stick with it, inspired by all the beautifully machine-quilted quilts I saw in magazines and at shows. Bit by bit I figured out what worked and was able to become quite comfortable with machine quilting.

The more I quilted, the more I noticed a change in my attitude. I no longer machine quilted just to get quilt tops completed (although that reason's still up there on my list!). I love the freedom machine quilting gives me—to design patterns as I go, to not mark if I don't want to, to use wonderful variegated threads and others that I couldn't possibly quilt with by hand. Machine quilting gives you a whole new way to express your creativity and have fun with your quilts. That's why I'm so excited to share with you all the wonderful ideas, techniques, and tips in this book. I know you'll enjoy machine quilting as much as I do.

We worked with some of the best machine quilters in the business to bring you the most up-to-date, useful information. You'll learn how to adjust your machine's tension so you get beautiful stitches every time. You can see how different specialty threads look when used for quilting before you invest in them. You'll feel confident in choosing the right batting for your project. And that's just for starters!

Our expert group of writers not only guide you through the basics, but they share all their best tips for success, too. And believe me, you will be successful. How do I know? Because while I was editing this book, I followed right along with each lesson and stitched many of the samples you see in this book.

I tried Julia Zgliniec's machine methods for corded trapunto, and I can't wait to put that technique to use in my own project. I bought water-soluble thread and stitched a trapunto design following Hari Walner's directions. I was amazed at how easy (and fast!) it is to create this very elaborate-looking effect. Once I followed Debra Wagner's advice on setting up my

machine's tension, I never had a single glitch in a stitch. And Laura Heine's suggestions for threads gave me the nudge I needed to branch out and try some of those fancy threads I've been admiring at the local quilt shop.

Even though I've been quilting on my machine for several years, I couldn't believe all the new ideas I was picking up—and using. Stitching through tissue paper, wearing latex gloves, basting by quilt tacking instead of safety pinning, even following a marked design with precision on a bed-size quilt—I feel as if I'm ready to tackle any kind of machine quilting I want to.

Of course my husband thinks I'm nuts. He can't believe that I've taken to sewing paper onto my quilts while wearing surgical gloves! But my results speak for themselves, and I know yours will, too. So have fun, get projects done, then go buy more fabric!

*Karen Soltys*

Karen Costello Soltys
Editor

# 20 Top Tips for Machine Quilting

**1** Experiment with different types of threads. What looks great for an antique reproduction quilt may not have the same impact on a watercolor quilt. New threads can open you up to new and creative ideas. Try them on a practice quilt sandwich first to be sure you're using the right needle and your machine tension is set accurately.

**2** Sewer's Aid, a silicone substance, can be applied to spools of metallic thread to help reduce risk of shredding.

**3** Combinations of techniques are often necessary. Outline quilting around appliqué motifs accentuates the appliqués, but stipple or echo quilting really flattens the background so they look fuller, almost stuffed. Filling background areas with continuous curving lines is easy and adds a lot of interest to the overall appearance of the quilt.

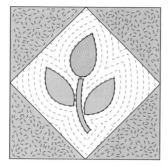
Echo and meandering quilting

**4** When you find your blood pressure rising and your fatigue increasing, remember to breathe while you are quilting! Take breaks every 30 minutes or so to do deep breathing and stretching exercises.

**5** Always pull the bobbin thread to the top of your quilt when you start a new line of stitching. Once that bobbin thread tail gets tangled underneath the quilt and stitched over repeatedly with free-motion stitches, it can be nearly impossible to remove.

Tug top thread to pull up bobbin loop

**6** When choosing quilting designs for a quilt that has a lot of seams, such as a Log Cabin, Drunkard's Path, or Rail Fence, back the quilt with an overall geometric print or a floral print with leaves and flowers that flow easily from one motif to another. That way, you can quilt from the back side of the quilt and follow the designs in the fabric. When shopping for these types of prints, run your fingertip around the shapes in any fabric you're considering.

If you can trace a line from one motif to the next without stopping, the fabric is suitable for free-motion, continuous-line quilting.

**7** After you've finished machine quilting a quilt, hang it on the wall or place it on a bed and photograph it with side lighting to emphasize the quilting. Or take it to a photographer for a really professional job. Every time you look at the photo you'll see what a great effect the stitching had on the overall appeal of the quilt and you won't hesitate to start the next project!

**8** Take time to practice or warm up before every machine-quilting session. Your fingers will be limber and your hands and foot will get back in rhythm. And who knows, you may even develop a new stitching pattern! It's the times when you're relaxed and not worrying about making a mistake on a "real" quilt that you have the freedom to develop your skills.

Practice free-motion quilting

**9** Space out your work sessions when doing a large quilt. It's not a marathon (unless it's Christmas Eve!), and machine quilting will look better if done with a fresh outlook—and a fresh body.

**10** Gingher makes curved embroidery scissors that are great for snipping threads while machine quilting. The curved design lets you get close to the surface without accidentally snipping into the quilt with the pointed tips of the scissors.

Curved embroidery scissors

**11** Pleat rather than roll a large quilt. It's much more flexible to work with. As Hari Walner puts it, a rolled quilt takes on the personality of a telephone pole. Imagine trying to move one of those through your machine!

**12** Free-motion quilting is *so* much easier when you're able to get a grip on your fabric—literally. Latex gloves work great, but if they get too hot, something as small and inexpensive as the little rubber needle grabbers used for hand quilting placed between your fingertips and the quilt top can provide great traction for moving your quilt.

**13** To save time (and your back), try using a quilt basting gun instead of pin basting. It's fast, easy, and each tack makes only one hole instead of two, like safety pins do. They don't get hung up on presser feet like safety pins

sometimes do. And you can stitch right up to the tack and your walking foot or darning foot won't mind a bit.

**14** No matter what basting method you use, make sure to baste very securely. You'll be handling, moving, and turning your quilt a lot, so don't risk having the layers shift. Baste close together, especially on a bed-size quilt— the bigger the quilt, the more you'll be maneuvering it.

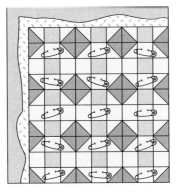
Pin baste securely

**15** Free-motion quilting does not necessarily mean stitching at the speed of light. Learn to move your quilt at a consistent pace that works with how fast you are moving the machine needle. Some quilters like to stitch quickly, but if you feel that your stitches are getting out of control (sort of like driving a car on ice), then slow down and take it easy.

**16** Lots of machine quilters use monofilament, especially when stitching in the ditch or for creating antique-looking cross-hatching. This thread can have a mind of its own. It's hard to see when threading the machine, and since it curls and twists in the

direction it wants to go, it comes unthreaded from the needle easily. To control monofilament, keep a piece of transparent tape on your machine bed. Whenever you clip the thread to move to another area, tape the end to your machine bed so it won't come unthreaded.

**17** Increase your regular stitch length a bit (more like 10 stitches per inch rather than 12) when you switch from piecing to machine-guided quilting. The stitches need to go through more layers and you don't want them to be totally buried.

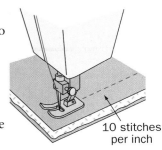
10 stitches per inch
Increase stitch length

**18** If you use a variety of different bobbin threads, keep the wound bobbins separated by type of thread in different bobbin boxes labeled with masking tape. For instance, if you use 50-weight threads for piecing and 40-weight threads for machine quilting, you'll have a hard time telling similarly colored bobbins apart unless they're labeled.

**19** After basting your quilt, roll the backing edges over the batting and pin them to the quilt top. By encasing the excess batting, you won't snag it on your machine or collect unwanted pet hair and stray threads.

**20** Machine quilting takes a lot of practice, just like any other skill. Don't get discouraged. Take a piece in progress to a quilt group meeting for a dose of encouragement.

20 TOP TIPS

# Preparing Your
## *Sewing Machine*

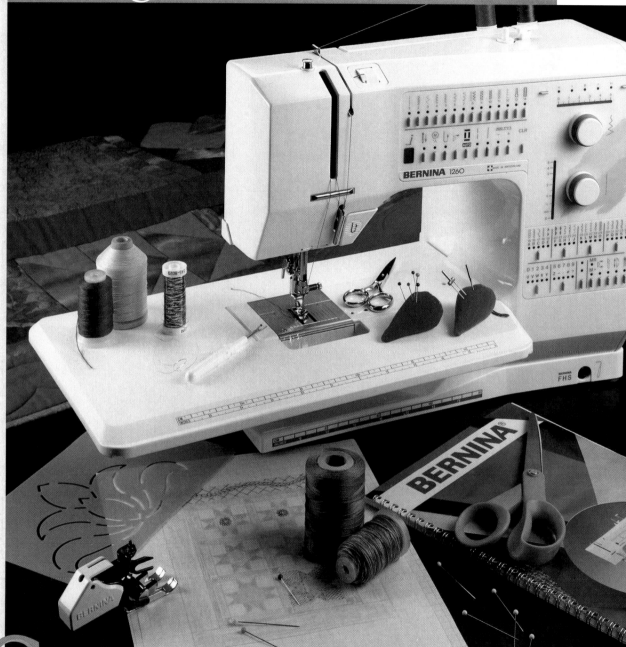

**G**et ready...get set...quilt! It's worth taking a few extra minutes to get ready and make sure everything on your machine is set just right. Preparing your sewing machine, using the proper equipment, and following basic maintenance will ensure great results. Don't worry—you don't need a degree in sewing machine mechanics. By following our easy guidelines, you can make sure you and your machine are ready to do some beautiful quilting together.

# Getting Ready

Refer frequently to your sewing machine owner's manual or instruction book. Every machine operates slightly differently from other brands and models. Our steps give basic directions, but your owner's manual will help you with the specifics.

Find all the basic accessories that came with your machine, including extra needles, oil, lint brush, spool pins, bobbins, and presser feet. Look for the darning foot and walking or even-feed foot. If you don't have these accessories, consult with your machine dealer.

Other accessories, such as an extension table and alternative spool pins, are necessities for the serious machine quilter. However, if you're a novice quilter, you may wish to practice quilting before investing in such supplies. That way, you'll be able to choose the supplies that best fit your quilting style.

## What You'll Need

**Sewing machine**

**Sewing machine owner's manual**

**Basic machine accessories**

**Automotive paste wax**

**Soft cotton cloth for cleaning**

**Extension table for portable machines**

**Alternative spool pin or stand designed for nontraditional threads**

**Walking foot or dual-feed mechanism**

**Darning or free-motion quilting foot**

 *For information on sewing machine needles, see "Choosing the Right Needle and Thread" on page 20.*

## Machine Preparation

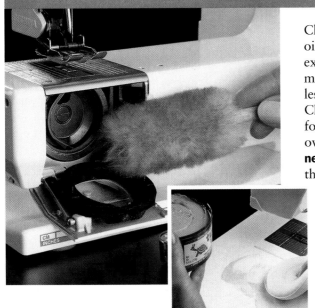

Clean your machine. Lint, dirt, and oil accumulate on the interior and exterior surfaces of the sewing machine. Keeping the machine spotlessly clean will keep your quilt clean. Clean and oil the bobbin case area following the instructions in your owner's manual. **Wipe lint from the needle and presser foot bars,** and dust the back, base, and bed of the machine.

**Wax the bed of the machine to make a smooth surface so the quilt slides easily during quilting.** Apply a small amount of automotive paste wax to the machine bed with a circular motion, keeping wax away from the feed dogs. Buff with a soft cloth to finish.

*Tip*

Keep lint out of the feed dogs with a sheepskin brush or canned air (available at art supply stores).

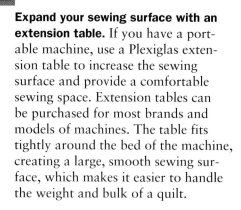

**Expand your sewing surface with an extension table.** If you have a portable machine, use a Plexiglas extension table to increase the sewing surface and provide a comfortable sewing space. Extension tables can be purchased for most brands and models of machines. The table fits tightly around the bed of the machine, creating a large, smooth sewing surface, which makes it easier to handle the weight and bulk of a quilt.

**Alternative spool stands make it possible to use a wide variety of threads, including those wrapped on cones or cores.** These threads may not fit your machine's spool pins, or if they do fit, they may unwind incorrectly. Alternative spool stands are available in many styles. The two most common are the traditional free-standing thread stands used for large cone threads and the upright spool pin adapter for machines that have horizontal thread pins.

For more information, see "Choosing the Right Needle and Thread" on page 20 and "No More Trouble with Tension!" on page 26.

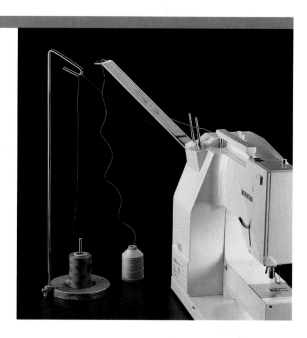

**For machine-guided quilting, use a walking foot or dual-feed mechanism for the best results.** The walking foot has a set of feed dogs to move the upper fabric layer in tandem with the machine's feed dogs, which must be in the raised position for machine-guided stitching. **On some machines (such as Pfaffs) the dual-feed mechanism is built into the machine and functions with a standard presser foot.** If you don't have a built-in feature, see your machine dealer for the walking foot model that will fit your machine.

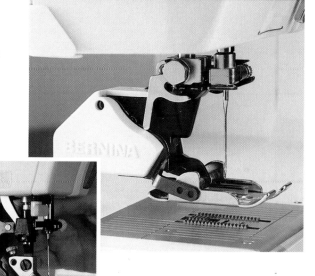

**For free-motion quilting you need a darning foot, which is a standard accessory with many machines.** Usually it's a small oval foot made of metal or plastic. Frequently this foot has an arm that fits the needle clamp to raise the foot and release the fabric. Read the owner's manual to correctly attach the foot.

**Generic variations of the darning foot are also available, and they generally come in styles to fit all standard sewing machines.** Choose a model with a clear plastic sole, such as the Big Foot brand, to increase visibility of the design line and stitching.

**Disengage or lower the feed dogs for free-motion quilting.** Check the owner's manual to determine how to do this on your machine. Typically, you can disengage the feed dogs by dropping them below the needle plate or covering them with a plastic or metal plate that snaps onto the machine bed.

Set the machine for the straight stitch. The stitch length setting will not affect the size of the stitches; however, it is best for the machine if you set the stitch length at zero or to the shortest possible stitch.

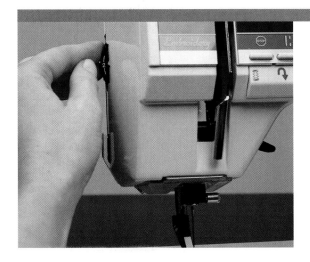

Many machines require that you adjust the pressure on the presser foot for free-motion quilting. Check your owner's manual under "Darning" to determine if this adjustment is required.

**Typically, you can adjust the pressure with a lever or dial,** which is usually located on the left side of the machine. Viking machines have outside dials, but the lever on many other brands is concealed inside the lightbulb door.

*Tip*

Metal darning feet have moving parts that attract lint. An occasional cleaning and oiling will keep the foot in top condition.

*Tip*

If you can't lower your feed dogs and you don't have a cover plate, cover them by taping a business card over them.

PREPARING YOUR SEWING MACHINE

13

# Setting Up a Machine -
## *Quilting Workspace*

As many of us head to our machines to complete our quilting projects, we often look for "magic" ways to make the job easier. Setting up a comfortable space to work in can make the difference between a frustrating machine-quilting session and a fun and successful one. You probably have most of the equipment you need around your home to get started. Once you have a basic setup, you can continue to adjust your arrangements until you're perfectly comfortable.

# Getting Ready

Find a place in your home that can be set up without being disturbed for the duration of your project. Eating may not be important to you while you are in the middle of an exciting project or facing an imminent deadline, but others in the household may not agree! So, if the dining room or kitchen table is the only space available, arrange a storage area nearby where your project can be stashed and retrieved quickly to work on again. Protect your quilt from soil and pets by covering it with a sheet when you are not working on it.

If you have another table available for your work area, set it up in a well-lit site, preferably near a window for natural light and to allow your eyes to rest and refocus.

## What You'll Need

**Large table or two smaller ones (one can be an adjustable ironing board)**

**Access to electrical outlets**

**Nonslip foot pedal surface**

**Adjustable-height chair**

**Adequate lighting**

**Stereo or radio**

**A place next to quilting table for drink, tissues, phone**

**Automotive paste wax or furniture polish**

# Workspace Setup

## The Right Space

**Locate an area of your home where you can set up a table or two that will allow you to have a quilt unfolded to the left of the machine and extended out the back of the machine.** You can use two tables, one to set the machine on and another to the left of or behind the first table to support your quilt. An ironing board can be used in place of a second table. Set it up behind or beside the machine table as needed to support the quilt. Make sure you have room to move around and push your chair back.

Be sure the spot you select has easy access to electrical outlets to prevent tripping over extension cords strung across the room.

## Sewing Tables

**Tip**

If using a ply wood work surface, wrap it with vinyl or a plastic drop cloth. Staple the plastic to the underside to create a smooth, slippery surface.

**If you do not have a large table, try two file cabinets with a piece of plywood, Formica countertop, or a hollow-core door on top.** The top surface of the board must be slippery to allow you to maneuver the quilt easily. The main requirement for a table is that it be stable and not vibrate when you sew. Card tables can work as a last resort, but most will wobble.

## Folding Tables

**Tip**

Attach a square of ¼" thick foam to the right of your machine with double-stick tape. Lay scissors, bobbins, and other notions on it and they won't vibrate off the table.

Folding tables, available at office supply stores, are convenient, reasonably priced, and can be folded and stored when not in use. **Place two folding tables side by side for supporting a large quilt.** They can be called into double-duty—use them for basting and cutting, too.

## More Table Solutions

You may have an unusual solution such as a Ping-Pong table, billiard table with a large board on top, breakfast counter, office desk, or other surface that can be adapted for machine quilting. **Some people even prefer to quilt standing up, so a kitchen countertop is perfect for them.** Be as creative with your work surface as you are with your quilts.

## Sewing Cabinet

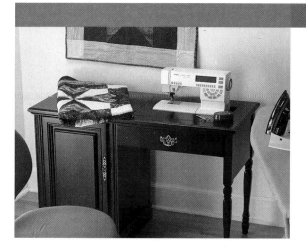

**A sewing table that you can drop your machine into is an ideal situation.** With this type of table, the surface of the machine bed is at the same level as the table, providing a large, smooth area for your quilt to move over. Even a small sewing machine cabinet with a table set up behind it is good, since it has a leaf to the left and everything is at the same level as the machine bed.

Wherever you choose to machine quilt, keep the machine foot pedal in place with a nonskid computer mouse pad or carpet grip.

## Adjustable Chair

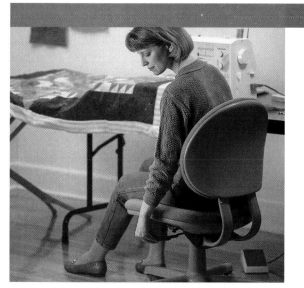

Find a chair that allows you to sit comfortably for long periods of time. **An adjustable chair is best, since you'll be able to move it to the exact height that's best for you.** Professional sewing chairs tilt the body slightly forward and raise and lower hydraulically.

A common problem for machine quilters is shoulder and back pain. Some like to quilt with the chair extra-low and some like it quite high. Experiment to see what position is most comfortable to you.

If you don't have an adjustable chair, you can raise your sewing tables to the perfect height with books or bricks.

## Lighting

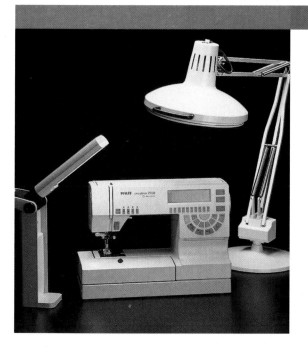

Good lighting is also a concern, especially if you do the majority of your quilting in the evening. Track lights are a good option, since they can be aimed in several directions: toward the sewing table, ironing board, cutting surface, and design wall, for example. **If your overhead lighting isn't suitable, try a portable light that you can direct, such as an Ott-Lite or a gooseneck work lamp.**

For daytime work, nothing is better than setting your table near a window so you can glance outside. Avoid direct sun on your work, however, as it will be very hard on your eyes, especially when it shines on the surface of the sewing machine or tabletop.

## Machine Setup

**Set your machine toward the right side of the table so you can take advantage of as much space as possible to the left of the machine.** If the machine is sitting above the table surface, attach the largest sewing machine bed you can find, or use an acrylic sewing surface made to fit around free-arm machines. (See Step 2 on page 12.)

Plug in the machine, making sure the cord is out of the way or taped to the floor so you do not trip on it.

## Comfort Quilting

*Tip*

Keep comfort supplies (beverages, tissues, TV remote control) away from your quilt. A TV tray table or nightstand nearby works well.

Turn on some music you enjoy, prepare your favorite beverage, hang out the "Do Not Disturb" sign, and sit down to machine quilt. If after a short time you experience discomfort in your shoulders or back, experiment with the height of the table or chair. You may need to adjust the height of either one, **or the solution may be as simple as taking periodic breaks.**

## The Ultimate Workspace

**If you can set up a permanent work area, consider adding a few more nice things to add to your use and enjoyment of the space.** An easy chair is great for relaxing and reading a new quilting magazine between work sessions—and your "loyal supporters" can use and enjoy it, too. Cabinets for fabric and quilt storage, racks for thread and notions, a desk for your computer, bookshelves for your books and patterns, and most important, a design wall to view works in progress, are all items that will add value and usefulness to your quilting space.

# The Quilter's
# Problem Solver

## Getting the Quilt to Move Easily

| Problem | Solution |
| --- | --- |
| **Quilt drags on surface of table.** | You don't have to invest a lot of money in a new table with a slick surface. Try a trash bag or two, instead. Lay the bags over your sewing table, then tape the edges to the underside of the table, and your quilt will slide around easily. |
| **Even with automotive paste wax or furniture polish, quilt still "sticks" to machine bed.** | Use latex surgical gloves, rubber fingers from the office supply store, or Quilterswrap (the sticky elastic bandages) to get a better grip on the quilt. These tools will help you get a grip on your quilt so you can move it around more easily, without having to press down firmly on it (which can cause some of the drag). |

**Skill Builder**

**Don't let less-than-ideal lighting hamper your quilting progress.**

Try one of these quick and easy (and often inexpensive) lighting fixes to prevent eyestrain:

❏ Inexpensive clamp-on hardware lights provide lots of light and can be clipped onto curtain rods or window frames.

❏ Lights on stands (sold for basement or garage workshops) are reasonably priced and provide excellent light.

❏ Long-necked lamps that screw onto the edge of the table can be aimed advantageously and stored when not in use.

❏ Even the floor lamp from the living room can be pressed into service, if necessary.

## Try This!

**Machine quilting sessions don't have to become tedious. A TV (with or without a VCR) or music can liven up the scene.**

❏ Most quilters only "watch" TV with their ears anyway. Place the TV next to your sewing table so you can glance at it occasionally—you'll help reduce eyestrain by looking at something farther away than your quilt every now and then.

❏ If you prefer music, play cassette tapes instead of the radio. Changing the tapes forces you to take a break and walk around. Plus, you can change music styles when you need a change of pace.

**MACHINE-QUILTING WORKSPACE**

# Choosing the Right
## *Needle & Thread*

Using a good-quality thread and the right type of machine needle is one of the easiest ways to guarantee success with machine quilting. But with dozens of decorative threads and nearly as many types of needles available, selecting the right combination for your quilt can be challenging. Let Laura Heine, quilt shop owner and award-winning machine quilter, guide you through the tangle of threads and needles. With her tips, you'll know right away which threads and needles to use for effortless machine quilting.

# Know Your Needles

Machine needles have five parts, and how those parts are constructed make some needles appropriate for machine quilting and others best for piecing.

The **shank,** the part that fits into the machine, is rounded on the front and flat on the back, so there's no danger of inserting it backward. Thread glides along the **groove,** which begins at the bottom of the shank and ends at the top of the eye. The **eye** is a highly polished hole where the thread is inserted. The **scarf** is the scooped-out area behind the needle. The larger the scarf, the easier it is to quilt with heavier-weight threads. The **point,** which can be very sharp or ballpoint, pierces the fabric.

At a glance, it's not always easy to differentiate one needle from another, so use the point codes printed on the packages to tell what use needles are designed for.

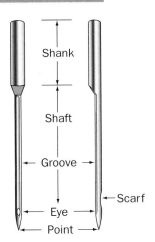

| Point Code | Use |
| --- | --- |
| H-J | Sharp point good for machine piecing |
| H-Q | Sharp, slimmer point better for machine quilting |
| H-E | Scarf designed for quilting with embroidery or decorative threads |
| MET | Eye designed for quilting with metallic or Mylar threads |

# Needle & Thread Selection

## Machine Needles

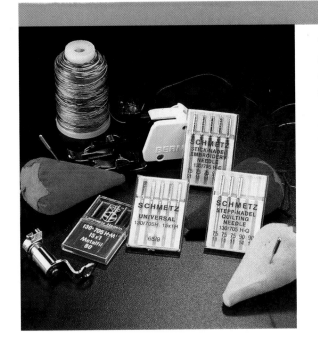

**You need to know two things about selecting the right needle for machine quilting: size and point code.** Sizes are shown with a dual numbering system (for example, 80/12 and 90/14), which indicates the European size followed by the American size. Unlike hand-sewing needles, the higher the number, the larger the needle. In general, you'll need a larger-size needle for machine quilting, since the needle needs to make a large enough hole in all three quilt layers for the thread to travel through and back.

The point code tells you what task a particular needle is best used for. See "Know Your Needles" above for details on deciphering the codes.

Dull needles damage fabric, so change your needle often—up to three times per twin-size quilt.

## Thread Basics

**Threads are numbered according to size, with the lightest-weight thread having the highest number.** A spool with the number 50/3 means it is a three-ply 50-weight thread. (Ply refers to the number of strands twisted together.) A 50/3 sewing thread is lighter or finer than a 40/3 quilting thread. The heavier the thread, the more it will show on your quilt top.

Refer to the following information for specific threads and what look they will give your quilt.

Thread weight

## Bobbin Threads

**Rayons, cottons, Jeans Stitch, and acrylics can all be used successfully as bobbin thread,** depending on what thread you use in the needle and the look you want for the quilt back. For instance, Jeans Stitch is much heavier than cotton thread, so the look will be more decorative.

Monofilament, metallics, and Mylar, on the other hand, are more difficult to work with in the bobbin. It's much easier to adjust tension when cotton is in the bobbin and the decorative thread is reserved for the quilt top.

See page 26 for information on adjusting tension.

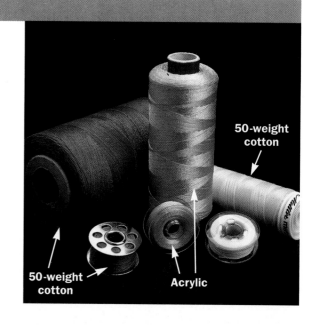

50-weight cotton

Acrylic

50-weight cotton

## Invisible Monofilaments

**Fiber content:** Nylon or polyester
**Best bets:** YLI or Sulky
**Weight:** .004 mm
**Appearance:** Old fashioned, hand-quilted look; use when invisible stitching line is desired
**Colors:** Smoke or clear
**Needle:** 90/14 embroidery
**Bobbin thread:** 50-weight cotton

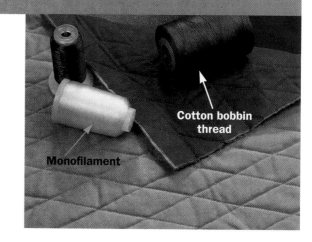

Cotton bobbin thread

Monofilament

## Cottons

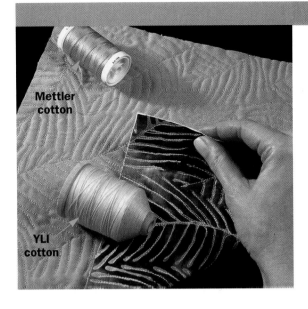

**Mettler cotton**

**YLI cotton**

**Fiber content:** 100 percent cotton
**Best bets:** Mettler and YLI
**Weight:** 50/3 for Mettler and 40/3 for YLI
**Appearance:** Traditional, utilitarian; great choice for bobbin thread. Note: YLI brand is glazed (for hand and machine quilting), so it has a somewhat more decorative look in machine quilting than Mettler thread since it's slightly stiffer and heavier.
**Colors:** Many solid colors
**Needle:** 80/12 sharp or 90/14 embroidery
**Bobbin thread:** 40- or 50-weight cotton or rayon

## Rayons

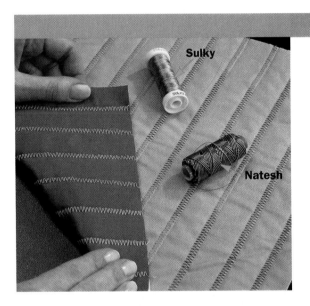

**Sulky**

**Natesh**

**Fiber content:** Rayon
**Best bets:** Sulky, Madeira, or Natesh
**Weight:** 30- and 40-weight
**Appearance:** Silky, decorative look; Natesh is heavier than other brands, which produces a slightly thicker line of stitching
**Colors:** All brands come in many solid and variegated colors
**Needle:** 75/11 or 90/14 embroidery
**Bobbin thread:** Sample stitched with 40-weight cotton; rayon is a good choice, too

## Metallics

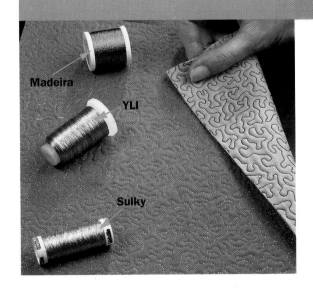

**Madeira**

**YLI**

**Sulky**

**Fiber content:** Metallic
**Best bets:** YLI, Sulky, or Madeira
**Weight:** Varies by brand; YLI is finer and easier to use than some brands
**Appearance:** Decorative thread; provides mild shine
**Colors:** Many solid and variegated colors
**Needle:** 90/14 embroidery or 80/12 Metallica
**Bobbin thread:** 50-weight cotton

**Tip**

Metallic threads break and shred fairly easily. To avoid this, put the spool in a baby food jar next to the machine and thread as usual.

**NEEDLE & THREAD**

## Acrylics

**Fiber content:** Acrylic
**Best bets:** YLI Ultrasheen
**Weight:** 40
**Appearance:** Fine decorative thread, used often for machine embroidery, creates a very fine quilting line
**Colors:** Many solid and variegated colors
**Needle:** 75/11 embroidery
**Bobbin thread:** Sample stitched with acrylic; 40-weight rayon or 50-weight cotton are good choices, too

## Jeans Stitch

*Tip*

The jeans/denim needle has a larger eye than the embroidery needle, which makes quilting with Jeans Stitch easier on tightly woven fabrics.

**Fiber content:** Polyester
**Best bets:** Only available from YLI
**Weight:** 30/3
**Appearance:** Heavy stitching line creates fun, decorative look; not suitable for bed quilts since thread is much stronger than the fabrics, and can cause shredding of fabrics if quilt is used
**Colors:** Many solid colors, plus one variegated (primary colors)
**Needle:** 90/14 embroidery or 90/14 jeans/denim
**Bobbin thread:** Sample stitched with Jeans Stitch; 40- or 50-weight cotton are good choices, too

## Mylar

*Tip*

Mylar threads break less easily than regular metallic threads, so try one on the next project that you want to shimmer!

**Fiber content:** Mylar or metallic
**Best bets:** Sulky Sliver or Madeira Jewel
**Weight:** Not applicable
**Appearance:** Flat, ribbonlike thread has a glitzy, reflective shine; looks wet or shimmery
**Colors:** Many solid colors
**Needle:** 90/14 embroidery or 80/12 Metallica
**Bobbin thread:** 40- or 50-weight cotton

**Sulky Sliver**

# The Quilter's
# Problem Solver

## Balancing Tension between Different Threads

| Problem | Solution |
|---|---|
| **With decorative thread on top and cotton in bobbin, bobbin thread always shows up on top of quilt.** | Reduce the tension of the needle thread slightly, until the top thread is pulled to the back of the quilt. If you need to reduce the tension too much to accomplish this, try a slightly heavier-weight thread in the bobbin, instead. For example, switch from 50- to 40-weight thread. With different thread weights and fiber contents, it's nearly impossible to adjust the tension so the top thread only shows on the top and the bobbin thread only shows on the bottom. |
| **If tension is adjusted so bobbin thread doesn't show on top, then top thread is visible on quilt back.** | Since you don't want bobbin thread showing on top, set the tension so the top thread goes slightly to the back and "hide" it by using a medium-value, busy print fabric for the quilt back. |

**Keep a quilt sandwich notebook for quick and easy thread/needle/tension reference.**

Each time you buy a new thread, try it out on a sample quilt sandwich before venturing on to a real quilt top. Record the name of the thread, the size and type of needle that worked best, what bobbin thread worked well, the tension setting, and even the batting choice right on the quilt sandwich. The next time you are considering using that thread, refer back to your sandwich notebook for all the details of your practice session. You won't have to start from scratch each time you begin to machine quilt a new project.

## Try This!

**Label the sections of a tomato pincushion with the different needle sizes.** When you change a needle due to a thread change (and not because it's "worn out" or dull), stick it in its corresponding size section of the pincushion. If you put it back in the original box, you'll quickly forget which of the needles in the box is new and which is used. A labeled pincushion, however, will make quick work of identifying both the size and point type of your needles.

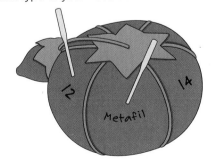

N E E D L E  &  T H R E A D

# No More Trouble
## *with Tension!*

Your machine's in a jam? Don't panic. Debra Wagner, award-winning machine quilter and sewing machine expert, will show you how to unravel the mysteries of the perfect machine-quilting stitch. Take a step-by-step look at the most common tension problems and discover their very simple solutions. Beautifully formed stitches are just a few easy steps away.

## Getting Ready

Refer to your sewing machine owner's manual for the correct way to thread the machine and load the bobbin. Most mistakes that get chalked up to tension problems happen because of simple threading errors.

Be a good detective and analyze a sample of the quilting stitch before looking for solutions. Examine the right and wrong sides of the sample for clues to help identify the problem. What looks wrong? When does the problem occur? The time you spend diagnosing the symptoms will make the solutions easier to find.

Last, keep in mind Debra's cardinal rule of solving machine problems: "When a dependable machine suddenly goes awry, chances are the problem is simple to solve."

### What You'll Need

**Sewing machine**

**Sewing machine owner's manual**

**Alternative spool pins designed for nontraditional threads**

**Assortment of machine needles**

**12" square practice quilt sandwich**

**Thread snips or embroidery scissors**

## Solving Tension Problems

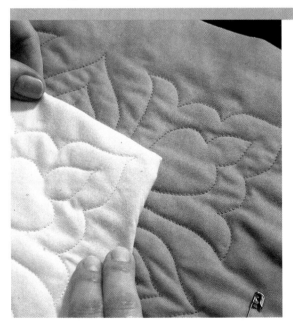

**The perfectly formed stitch is characterized by smooth, neat threads on both sides of the quilt.** The thread doesn't pull on the fabric or cause puckers. There are no loops or thread knots on either side of the quilt. Perfect stitching is easiest to achieve on machine-guided quilting because the machine makes the best stitches when sewing forward. Perfect tension is difficult to maintain when free-motion quilting, since the constant changing of stitching direction affects the stitch formation. It is acceptable for small dots of needle thread to appear on the wrong side of the quilt when free-motion quilting.

**2**

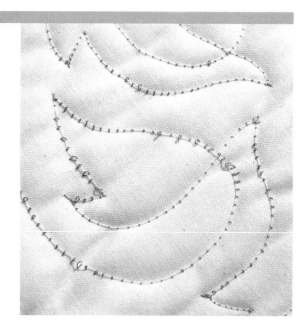

**One common stitch problem is too much needle thread being visible on the back of the quilt.** The thread may be as insignificant as small dots, but sometimes it forms loops or knots, and at its worst can cause a thread jam. To correct this situation, rethread the machine with the presser foot *raised*. Then *lower* the presser foot to stitch a new sample.

If rethreading doesn't correct the problem, check to make sure the needle tension wasn't accidentally moved to a lower-than-normal setting. Finally, try tightening the upper thread tension. See Step 8 on page 30 for instructions.

**3**

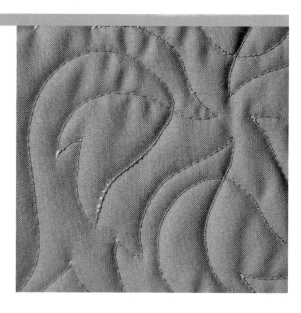

**Another stitch problem occurs when the bobbin thread is visible on the quilt top, appearing as small bumps.** Try to correct the problem by:
• Raising the presser foot and rethreading the machine.
• Checking that the needle tension wasn't moved to a higher setting.
• Making sure you're using the correct bobbin for your machine.
• Loosening top needle tension or checking the bobbin tension to determine if it needs to be adjusted or repaired. *If indicated in the owner's manual,* tighten the bobbin tension. See Step 9 on page 30 for instructions.

**4**

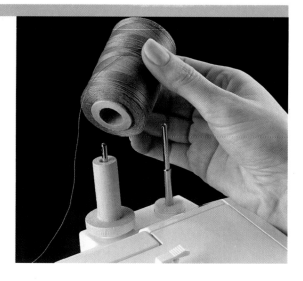

*Tip*

If your machine holds thread horizontally, try taping a wooden dowel to the side of the machine, so spools can be used vertically.

Tension problems are frequently caused by the top thread not feeding freely. Check to see if the thread is caught on the quilt behind the machine. Or perhaps it's catching on a clip or notch on the spool edge. **The solution may be to use an alternative spool pin, such as this wooden one, or a thread stand,** which will allow a large spool to spin freely or a small spool to spin steadily. See Step 2 on page 12 for additional types of spool holders.

**Sometimes stitch quality alternates between good and bad.** The causes of erratic stitching are the most difficult to diagnose and correct. Uneven stitching can form loops on the top or bobbin side of the stitching and is frequently characterized by puckered or skipped stitches and broken threads.

Rewind the bobbin, making sure you're using the correct bobbin for your machine brand and model. If stitch quality doesn't improve, replace the needle, checking to make sure the needle is correctly in the clamp.

*Tip*

Skipped stitches are almost always caused by the needle and thread combination. Poor tension doesn't cause skipped stitches.

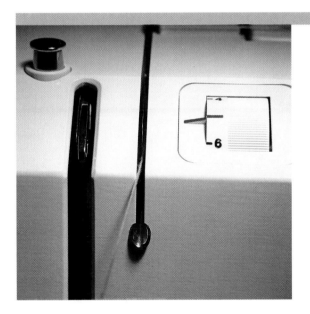

Erratic stitches can be caused by lint. Clean the machine thoroughly. Check both the bobbin area and the needle tension disks.

Needle tension disks can fill with lint and become clogged. When tension disks are clogged, they will not work as well. **Most machines have a two-sided needle tension assembly. Try rethreading on the opposite side of the tension disk.** Often, using the opposite side of the disk will temporarily correct the problem. However, if you suspect there is a problem with one side of the tension disks, have your machine cleaned or repaired.

*Tip*

Try canned air for forcing out any lint without damaging the tension disk mechanism.

Erratic stitching can also be caused by the spool or bobbin. **Occasionally the spool or bobbin can become "bruised" by rough handling. The bruise occurs when the threads on the outer layer of the spool or bobbin are forced into the inner layers.** The threads become wedged together, causing a momentary tightening of the thread tension as it unwinds in the damaged area. The effect is easy to spot because it happens at regular intervals. The thread may require an alternative spool pin or stand to help the thread feed freely.

*Tip*

When tension problems have you in knots, take a break. Make a cup of tea, and relax before returning to the problem.

**NO MORE TROUBLE WITH TENSION!**

**8**

The top tension is the easiest to adjust. Begin by writing down the original number or setting. Adjust with finesse, taking small steps, a half-number at a time. Small adjustments can make a large difference. **Remember, the lower the number, the looser the tension. Or, "Right, tight. Left, loose."**

Stitch on a practice quilt sandwich to assess the improvement after every adjustment. If the problem is not corrected within a number or two of the original setting, look for problems other than tension control.

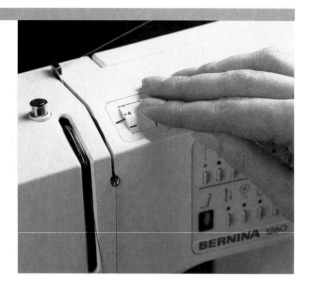

If you regularly use a thicker bobbin thread for decorative work, purchase a spare bobbin case and adjust it specifically for specialty thread.

**9**

Don't adjust the bobbin case tension unless it is explained in the owner's manual. On many machines the bobbin case tension is factory-set for regular sewing thread and shouldn't need adjustment unless the machine needs repair.

**The tension on the bobbin case is controlled by a *very* small screw and a curved metal band, called the spring, that wraps around the bobbin case.** Problems arise because there is no way to mark the original setting. Once you have adjusted the tension it is difficult to reinstate the original setting.

Spring

Screw

**10**

Check your bobbin tension before changing it. If your machine has a removable bobbin case, load a full bobbin in the case. **Hold the thread in one hand, suspending the bobbin case over the other hand. The bobbin case should drop gently down the thread as you "jiggle" the thread.** If it drops quickly, the tension screw is loose. Tighten it and test again.

Another way to assess the bobbin tension is to thread the machine, except for the needle, and lower the presser foot. Load the bobbin. Tug on the bobbin and the top thread to compare the tensions. They should be approximately even.

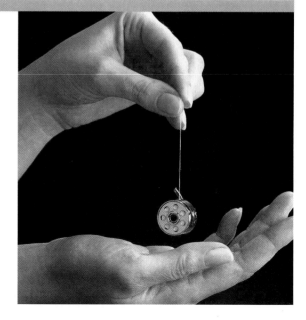

# The Quilter's
# Problem Solver

## Locating Tension Problems

Most tension problems aren't caused by the thread tension assembly and therefore can't be solved by adjusting the tensions. Surprisingly, many major thread tension problems originate with threading or the needle. When your machine is having tension troubles, it's a good idea to follow the TNT rule: Thread, Needle, Tension. This order of checking the machine looks at the most common problems first.

| Problem | Solution |
| --- | --- |
| Incorrect threading—in machine or bobbin. | Always begin by completely rethreading the needle and the bobbin case. This frequently solves the problems. Sometimes, the problem is as simple as a bobbin loaded backward or the needle thread catching on the edge of the spool. |
| Damaged or wrong size needle. | Is the needle in the machine correctly, with the high and flat sides facing in the correct directions? If so, perhaps a different size or type of needle is needed. Change the needle, referring to "Know Your Needles" on page 21 for the right needle and thread combination. |
| Problematic tension. | When all other potential causes have been eliminated, then adjust the tension. |

## Skill Builder

### Control tension while free-motion quilting.

Tension problems are most noticeable on free-motion quilting. The constant change in stitching direction can adversely affect the stitch formation. For the best stitch quality, try a straight-stitch needle plate. The small needle hole opening improves the stitch formation, corrects tension problems, and prevents skipped stitches. The improvement is the most evident on machines with 6 mm or larger zigzag widths. Not every machine has an optional straight-stitch plate, and you must purchase the accessory according to both brand name and model number of your machine.

## Try This!

**Unbalanced thread tensions can produce a new look for your machine stitching.** One interesting effect uses a tightened top tension to simulate a hand-quilting stitch. Use invisible thread in the needle and a mismatched polyester thread in the bobbin. Tighten the top tension to pull a small dot of bobbin thread to the right side of the quilt. Tighten the top tension one number at a time until you achieve the desired effect. You can loosen the bobbin slightly to enhance the effect. The stitch works best with machine-guided stitching.

NO MORE TROUBLE WITH TENSION!

# Marking
# *Quilting Designs*

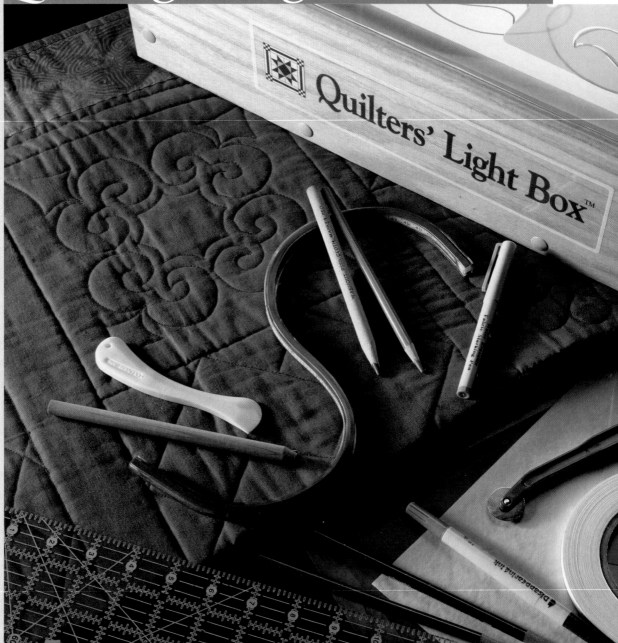

**M**arking a quilt top is surely one of the least favorite parts of the quiltmaking process for many quilters—partly because it's time-consuming, and partly because it's difficult to find the perfect marking tool for the job. In short, you want a marking method that is easy to do, easy to see, and easy to remove. As a machine quilter, you have options not available to hand quilters that do just that—make marking easier so you can get to the fun part of quilting faster.

# Getting Ready

You may not need to mark any designs on the quilt if you are going to do free-motion techniques like stipple, echo, or meander quilting. If you decide to do set patterns, it's a good idea to mark more complicated designs on the quilt top before you baste it to the batting and backing. For simpler designs, you can baste first and mark areas as you get to them. With flatter, low-loft battings being used today, there is usually no problem with marking after the layers are basted together.

If you don't already have a variety of marking tools, you may want to read through the different steps before purchasing anything new. You won't need all the tools listed—just those needed for the type of marking you intend to do. Good lighting is essential so that you don't mark the quilt top too heavily. A working surface that's countertop height will help prevent a stiff back when doing extensive marking.

## What You'll Need

**Hera**

**Masking tape**

**Marking pencils**

**Stencils—purchased or self-made with Mylar and a double-blade X-Acto knife**

**Graph paper**

**For stitch-through quilting:**

> **Vellum or tissue paper, baking parchment, preprinted quilting paper, tracing paper, lightweight interfacing or stabilizer**

**Large sheets of clear plastic**

**Tracing wheel and Saral transfer paper**

**Fine-point permanent black marking pen**

**Con-Tact paper**

**Large sewing machine needle, sandpaper, and cinnamon or cornstarch**

## Marking a Quilt

**Choosing a marking method will depend on the fabrics used in the quilt and the type of quilting you plan to do.** Straight lines can easily be marked with a hera (see page 74) or masking tape, while feathers and other intricate designs require other tools, such as pencils, stencils, or designs marked on paper. And some methods show up better on dark fabrics than others. You may not need all the supplies listed above, but it's always wise to test different methods before marking. Keep in mind the goal of creating a marking that is both easy to see for stitching *and* easy to remove afterward.

**Tip**

Also determine whether you plan to wash your finished quilt or not. Some markings can only be removed with washing, while others don't require that step.

## 2

**Audition overall quilting designs by drawing the quilt top on graph paper. Draw quilting designs on tracing paper and place them over the graph-paper quilt.** Or, pin the quilt top to the design wall and create a full-size quilting diagram on tracing paper, lightweight interfacing, tear-away stabilizer, or clear plastic. Then you can change lines until you achieve the results you want without making any marking errors on the quilt itself.

**After the plan is finished, trace the lines onto the quilt using Saral transfer paper and a tracing wheel, pen, or pencil.**

## 3

Quilt shops carry many markers, and you may want to experiment with several to see which fit your needs. Pencils come in silver and gold, white chalk or white wax-type, and regular lead. Wide colored leads are hard to keep sharp and also need to be washed out, whereas a thin mechanical lead pencil line or a silver or white pencil line will be covered with stitching and will not need to be removed. **Test to see which markers will be the most visible with the lightest amount of pressure applied while marking. Lines should be thin enough to disappear under the stitching.**

## 4

**Tip**

The bridges in a stencil will create breaks in your marked lines. Connect them with your pencil to avoid confusion while stitching.

The various markers are used with several types of aids for transferring a pattern to your quilt top. One of them is a commercially cut plastic stencil that has narrow channels with bridges in them to keep the stencil together. **Run the marking pencil through the channels at an angle so that the lead moves smoothly over the fabric instead of puckering it.** Look for stencils with designs that have continuous sewing lines so that you do not need to stop and start too often.

To make your own stencil, purchase a sheet of Mylar or template plastic at a craft store or quilt shop. **Draw a design on the plastic with a permanent marker, and use a double-bladed X-Acto knife to cut the channels. Leave bridges in the lines no further apart than 2 inches.**

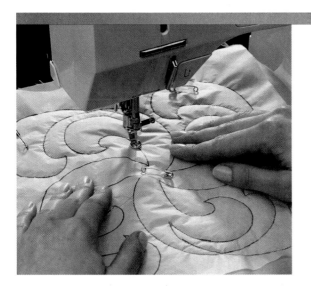

**Another way to cut a stencil is to draw a motif that can be drawn around.** Overlap, rotate, or place motifs side by side to create continuous stitching lines.

A very easy marking method is drawing designs on paper, rather than directly on the quilt. Vellum or baking parchment are good choices. They tear away easily after you sew through them, and they're transparent enough that you can place them easily. Vellum comes in 60-foot rolls—ideal for borders and blocks.

Mark quilting lines on the paper with a stencil, run sheets through a computer printer, or trace printed designs. **Pin the pattern securely to the quilt, and use a short stitch length to stitch through it so it will be easier to remove.**

*Tip*

You can also purchase vellum that is preprinted with quilting designs.

**You can also cut quilting motifs from Con-Tact paper and stick them onto the quilt top.** Stitch ⅛ inch away from the Con-Tact paper so adhesive won't get on the sewing machine needle. You can reposition a motif several times before the stickiness wears off. Test Con-Tact paper on a sample quilt sandwich (same batting and fabric as your quilt) to determine whether it will cause bearding. **If you're sewing straight lines, such as in cross-hatching, masking tape can be used in the same way.**

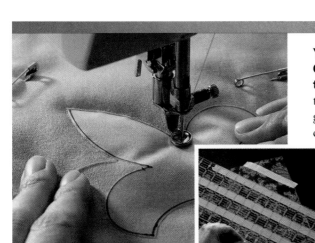

*Tip*

Before using a fresh piece of Con-Tact paper or masking tape, stick it onto a scrap of fabric to remove the excess adhesive.

MARKING QUILTING DESIGNS

## 8

Sometimes a quilt top is so "busy" that there are no continuous seam lines or consistent design elements to follow for the quilting. **A fun solution is to use a large floral print or plaid for the back of the quilt and stitch along the pattern of that fabric so the front of the quilt will be unified by an overall quilting design.**

You can even try a heavier thread in the bobbin case (the thread that will show on the quilt top) than would be possible if sewing from the front. You may need to loosen the tension on the bobbin case screw to allow for the larger thread. See page 30 for specifics on adjusting bobbin tension before you try this!

## 9

Borrowing a trick from old-time hand quilters, you can transfer designs to a quilt top with pouncing powder. **Design a quilting motif for a quilt block by folding paper as you would for a paper snowflake and drawing lines on one section. Put a size 100/16 or 120/18 needle in the sewing machine, unthread the machine, and sew on the lines through all of the layers of the paper.**

For a border design, accordion-fold a strip of paper and follow the same procedure.

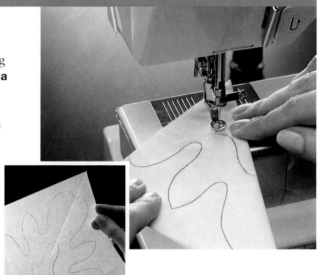

## 10

Use sandpaper to smooth the holes on the back of the paper. This will also make the holes a bit bigger so more powder can go through them. **Lay the perforated paper on the quilt top and rub cinnamon or cornstarch through the holes, depending on the color of the fabrics.** Carefully remove the paper pattern and connect the dots of powder with a marking pencil. If you don't trace over the dots with pencil, they'll rub off and you'll be left with no markings.

## Where Are My Markings?

| Problem | Solution |
|---|---|
| **Pencil marks do not show.** | Mark patterns on vellum paper. You can mark as dark as you want on paper without having to worry about erasing or washing out the marking. Pin paper patterns to the quilt and stitch through them using a short stitch length. Remove paper carefully. |
| **Marking rubs off before you get to it.** | Larger-size quilts go through a lot of handling for machine quilting. Try marking only one section at a time to avoid wasting time redoing worn-away markings. |

### Test marking methods on a quilt series.

For an interesting series, make three small wallhangings of a simple design and quilt them in three distinctly different patterns.

❏ Do a fancy curved design on one, stitching through a vellum pattern.

❏ Stitch an overall grid on another, using masking tape to lay out the straight lines.

❏ Quilt a flowing, gracefully curving design on one with the design planned on clear plastic and transferred to the quilt with a tracing wheel and Saral paper.

You'll build your skills in marking, machine quilting, and quilt design, plus have a wonderful group of small quilts to display.

## Try This!

**Make a quick marking reference for yourself.** Gather all of the marking pens and pencils you can find, possibly pooling pencils with quilting friends at a guild meeting. Write the names of the markers on a piece of patchwork made up of various colors and patterns of fabric. (Orphan blocks from previous projects will work great.) Layer the patchwork with batting and backing fabric, and stitch over part of the words. See how well the marking shows on the various fabrics and how well the stitching covers the markings.

# The Basics
## of Batting

**W**hen it comes to selecting batting, a quilter's life is no bed of roses. On the plus side, there is an enormous variety of battings from which to choose. The dilemma, of course, is how to figure out which one is right for you and your project. If you find yourself in a state of confusion while standing in front of the selection at your local quilt shop, read on to find some easy pointers that can steer you to the best batting for your particular project.

# Basic Batting Vocabulary

There are several terms you need to be familiar with to choose a batting.

*Bearding:* Batting fibers that work themselves out from the middle of the quilt and through the top and backing fabrics, creating a fuzzy look.

*Bonding:* A coating on the surface of the batting to hold the cotton or polyester fibers together. Bonding helps prevent bearding but makes the batting harder to needle. This isn't of much concern when machine quilting, but for hand quilting you can remove some of the bonding by presoaking the batting.

*Drape:* The amount of softness versus stiffness in a batting. Think about this when you compare a wallhanging to a bed quilt. You want your wallhanging to be relatively stiff so it doesn't sag, but you want a bed quilt to wrap comfortably around you.

*Loft:* The amount of puffiness (airy thickness) in a batting.

*Needlepunching:* A technique used to hold the batting fibers together to prevent bearding in polyester or fiber migration in cotton batting.

*Scrim:* A thin polyester sheet, almost like a skin, that is bonded to one side of a cotton batting to help keep it flat and durable.

*Shrinkage:* The amount a quilt's batting will reduce in size when laundered. Shrinkage will affect the look and size of a finished quilt and may help you decide whether you will prewash a certain type of batting before using it in your quilt.

# What You Need to Know about Batting

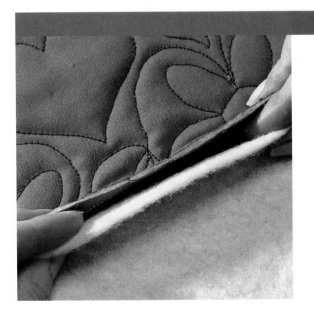

## Cotton

**Cotton shrinks when washed, giving an antique, crinkled look to your quilt.** If you are not prewashing, air-fluff your batting in the dryer to relax it and take out any large wrinkles or folds. If you want a smoother look in the finished quilt, prewash cotton batting according to the manufacturer's instructions. (When it says "don't agitate," don't agitate!)

Cotton battings with a scrim lie flatter, are stiffer, and are slightly more durable. Cotton beards less than polyester, and the bearding may resemble powder more than fibers. Cotton batts also hug the quilt top and backing fabrics, which prevents shifting or slipping of layers during machine quilting.

Instead of washing cotton batting, toss it in the dryer on high heat to preshrink it. You'll avoid the risk of its being shredded in the washing machine.

## Cotton-Polyester Blend

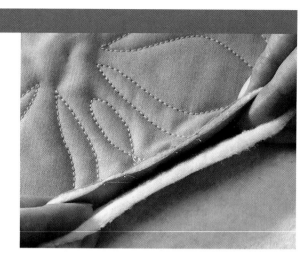

**Cotton-polyester blend battings have most of the characteristics of a cotton batting, but with the added advantage that they are easier to handle—like a more forgiving polyester batting.** They will beard slightly more than 100 percent cotton. One big advantage is that they can be quilted at larger intervals than all-cotton battings. The amount of shrinkage depends on the mix of polyester and cotton. The higher the cotton content, the more it will shrink.

## Polyester

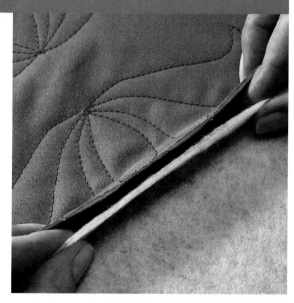

Polyester does not need to be prewashed, but air-fluffing in the dryer will relax it and take out any large creases or folds. Expect some bearding with a 100 percent polyester batt, although many manufacturers are trying out new bonding methods for the fibers to reduce bearding. Polyester is very durable and warm, since its synthetic fibers trap body heat. **Loft selection varies from ultra-thin Thermore (shown here) to a puffy extra-loft batt, but medium loft is best for machine quilting.** Polyester batts can be quilted at much larger intervals than cotton batts, but they don't hug the fabrics as cotton does.

 *Tip*

Make sample machine-quilted sandwiches with different types of batting. Write the type of batting on the top layer for easy reference.

## Wool

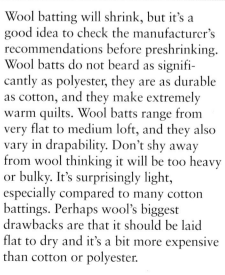

Wool batting will shrink, but it's a good idea to check the manufacturer's recommendations before preshrinking. Wool batts do not beard as significantly as polyester, they are as durable as cotton, and they make extremely warm quilts. Wool batts range from very flat to medium loft, and they also vary in drapability. Don't shy away from wool thinking it will be too heavy or bulky. It's surprisingly light, especially compared to many cotton battings. Perhaps wool's biggest drawbacks are that it should be laid flat to dry and it's a bit more expensive than cotton or polyester.

*Tip*

Some quilt shops and mail-order catalogs offer batting sampler packs so you can try them before deciding on one for a quilt.

## Silk

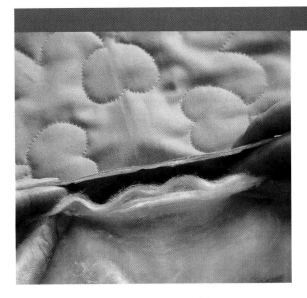

Silk batting is actually many light-weight layers of silk "leaves." To use it, you peel off the layers, pull and fluff the fibers, and pat them into place on your quilt top. **There are also sheets of silk batting that you treat just as you would cotton or polyester, but they must be handled with extreme care so they don't degrade into piles of fluff.** Silk batting is considerably more expensive than cotton, polyester, or wool, but it's extremely drapable, making it perfect for lightweight quilts and machine-quilted garments.

Always launder batting or finished quilts following the recommended guidelines on the batting package—they can vary greatly based on the brand or content.

## Drape

Lightweight, low-loft battings, especially polyester ones, have the most drapability. They're soft and flexible. **Cotton battings, even low-loft varieties, can be a bit stiffer, which is good for wallhangings,** table runners, and other items you want to hang or drape while retaining the original shape. Bed quilts, lap quilts, and garments, on the other hand, feel best when they have some drape. They feel less stiff and are nicer to snuggle in. **While cotton batts can be stiffer when new, washing them usually gives them more drape and a softer, more old-fashioned appearance.**

## Bearding

Bearding can happen with any batting other than 100 percent cotton. Little bits of the batting creep through the quilt top or backing, creating unsightly fuzzy little balls on the surface of the quilt. **Bonded batting helps prevent bearding, but if you are fearful about the possibility, stick with cotton batting.**

If a quilt beards, carefully snip off the offensive bits of batting. Pulling them off with tape only makes matters worse.

**THE BASICS OF BATTING**

## Quilting Spacing

**The length of the fibers used in a quilt batt determine how close you will need to quilt your layers.** Polyester batts usually can be quilted 4 to 5 inches apart (about the width of the palm of your hand) without risking fiber migration. Cotton, wool, and silk batts may require closer quilting (as close as 1½ to 2 inches apart over the entire quilt). Check the manufacturer's recommendation before settling on a quilting design.

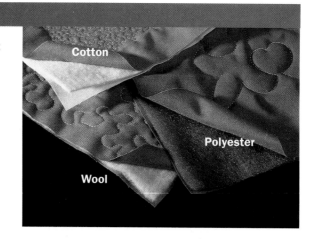

Cotton

Polyester

Wool

## Shrinkage

**Tip**

Machine quilt a few sample sandwiches, some with prewashed fabrics and batts, and some with unwashed fabrics and batts.

Although the quilt in the photograph is hand quilted, the amount and effects of shrinkage are similar. **The fabrics in this quilt were prewashed, but the 80 percent cotton/20 percent polyester batting was not. Since the batting shrunk about 5 percent, the result of washing the quilt after it was completed is a new quilt with the look and feel of a much loved—and much older—family heirloom.** The best way to deal with shrinkage in a batting is to gain first-hand experience.

After washing

Before washing

## Loft/Warmth

**The loft of batting you choose will affect the overall look of your quilt, even though the batting is hidden between the layers.** High-loft batts are suitable for tied comforters and machine trapunto (see page 102), while low-loft batts are better for hand and machine quilting. A low-loft batt will give your quilt more of an antique quilt appearance. If your concern is for warmth, don't feel that a high-loft batt is the only way to go. Polyester is very warm, as is wool. Cotton is a good year-round choice.

# The Quilter's Problem Solver

## Batting Selection Guide

| Questions to Guide Your Selection | Types of Batting | | | | |
|---|---|---|---|---|---|
| | Cotton | Cotton/Polyester | Polyester | Wool | Silk |
| **How do you plan to hold the three layers together?** | | | | | |
| Hand quilting | ✔ | ✔ | ✔* | ✔* | ✔ |
| Machine quilting | ✔ | ✔ | ✔* | ✔* | ✔ |
| Tying | ✔† | ✔ | ✔ | ✔ | |
| **How do you want your completed quilt to look?** | | | | | |
| Old-fashioned and flat | ✔ | ✔ | ✔* | ✔* | ✔ |
| Some texture and loft | | ✔ | ✔* | ✔* | ✔ |
| Puffy and cozy | | | ✔§ | ✔§ | ✔ |
| **How much time do you plan to spend quilting this quilt?** | | | | | |
| As long as it takes | ✔ | ✔ | ✔* | ✔* | ✔ |
| Only as much as I have to | ✔† | ✔ | ✔*‡ | | ✔ |
| Just enough to hold it together | ✔† | | | | |
| **How will you use this quilt?** | | | | | |
| With care on a bed | ✔ | ✔ | ✔* | ✔* | ✔ |
| As a piece of clothing | ✔† | ✔ | ✔* | ✔* | ✔ |
| As a wallhanging | ✔† | ✔ | ✔ | | |
| Over the back of the couch as a nap quilt | ✔ | ✔ | ✔ | ✔ | |
| Carried around by a small child | ✔† | ✔ | ✔ | | |
| As an entry in a quilting competition | ✔ | ✔ | ✔* | ✔* | ✔ |

*High-loft not appropriate. †Look for needle-punched cotton. ‡Low-loft not appropriate.
§ Look for high-loft batt.

# Layering & Basting
## *for Machine Quilting*

**B**asting, although tedious, is an important step in the quilting process. There are several ways to baste the layers of your quilt sandwich together, and any of them will work well as long as you do them carefully. Adequate basting is essential for machine work because you will be rolling and unrolling the quilt many times and you do not have a hoop in which to smooth the layers before starting a new section. Try out a few basting methods to see which one works best for you.

# Getting Ready

Having a large workspace is critical for good basting. The floor will work if you have either a wood or tile surface or low-pile carpeting. A large surface like a cutting table is ideal because you can walk around all sides of the table to reach sections more easily, and you can baste most quilts one half at a time—the whole quilt doesn't have to fit on the table at once. Two office or school tables pushed together work well, too. Four long boards held together with C-clamps and propped up on chairs is another alternative.

Gather all your supplies and press the quilt top carefully with seam allowances smooth, not twisted. Make sure your batting is preshrunk if it is cotton or cotton/poly, or fluffed if it is polyester. Seam and press the backing fabric, leaving a minimum of 2 inches extra on all sides of the quilt top. Put on some music or invite a friend over for coffee and see if she'll help.

## What You'll Need

**Masking tape**

**Long straight pins**

**Nickel-plated safety pins (curved or straight), *or* quilt basting gun, *or* milliner's needle and thread**

**Kwik Klip or grapefruit spoon for safety pins (optional)**

**Optional table basting:**

   **Large office clamps, *or* plastic tablecloth clamps**

**Optional frame basting:**

   **Four long boards (1" × 4")**

   **Four 3" or 4" C-clamps for boards**

   **Square ruler (8" or 15")**

   **Four chairs to hold frame**

   **Thumbtacks**

# Layering & Basting

After piecing the backing, **tape the quilt backing fabric wrong side up to the table or floor, taping the corners first and then the sides every 12 inches or so.** Tape opposite sides first, then tape the ends to avoid distorting the fabric. Pull the fabric taut with the masking tape, but do not stretch it or you will have puckering problems on the top later.

*Tip*

Pets especially enjoy floor projects, so when you take a break from basting to rest your back, cover the quilt layers with a sheet.

## 2

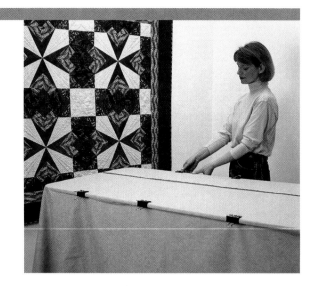

If you do not have a working surface as large as the quilt, place half of the backing on a table, or for a very large piece, place the middle third of the backing on a table. Tape any edges that you can. **Use office clamps or tablecloth clips to hold other areas of the backing fabric to the table edges.** When you have basted the area on the table (following the directions in later steps), move the quilt layers so the next unbasted area is on the tabletop. Reclamp and tape the backing to the table, and continue stitching the next section.

## 3

Another option for basting is to do it on a frame, rather than a flat surface. If you are using boards and C-clamps, lay out the boards in a square or rectangle that is a few inches smaller than the quilt backing. (Your backing should be extra large for this method.) C-clamp the boards together at the corners using a square rotary cutting ruler to check that the corners are 90 degree angles. **Prop the frame of boards on the backs of four chairs. Thumbtack the backing to all four boards so it is taut.**

## 4

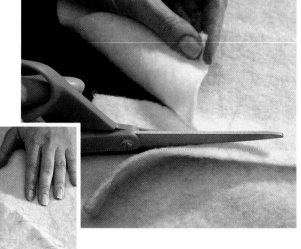

If your batting isn't large enough, you can piece it. **Overlap the edges of the two pieces slightly, and cut through both layers.** Remove the narrow strips that were cut off, leaving exactly matched edges butted together. **Whipstitch the edges together by hand,** or zigzag stitch them on the machine with white or off-white thread to prevent show-through. Be sure this is done well to avoid holes in the batting when the quilt is washed later.

Lay the batting on top of the backing fabric and pat gently to smooth it out. Cut batting to the same size as the backing fabric. Using a long tape measure, find the center or midpoint along each edge of the batting. **Place a long straight pin in the batting at the centers of each edge of the backing so you can match the midpoints of the quilt top edges to them.**

Refer to "The Basics of Batting" on page 38 for guidelines on preparing your batting before layering it into your quilt.

Fold your quilt in half in each direction or measure it to find the midpoint on each edge. **Then lay the quilt top right side up over the batting, matching the centers of each side to the pins in the batting.** Smooth out all ripples in the quilt top and check to see that the borders are square and straight.

This step is made much easier with the help of a family member or friend.

While traditional thread basting can be used for machine quilting (see Steps 9 and 10 on page 48), it isn't the best choice if you plan to quilt heavily with free-motion quilting. Pin basting is preferred by many quilters, since pins are easily removed as they near the machine needle. **For pin basting, place safety pins in the center area of the quilt and work out to the edges of the quilt, pinning every 3 to 4 inches.**

If your quilt is large, your hand will get tired from closing all the pins, **so use a Kwik Klip or grapefruit spoon to help close them.**

It's easier to wait to close the pins until after you've released the masking tape, clips, or thumbtacks from the backing edges.

LAYERING & BASTING

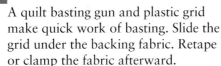

**Tip**

Remove tacks from the wrong side, pulling them away from the quilt so you have a long shank to cut and won't risk clipping the quilt.

## 8

A quilt basting gun and plastic grid make quick work of basting. Slide the grid under the backing fabric. Retape or clamp the fabric afterward. **Holding the tacking gun perpendicular to the quilt, pierce the quilt layers, making sure the point goes through a space in the grid. Shoot a tack into the quilt and pull out the gun.** Place a tack every 3 to 4 inches, moving the grid around under the quilt as necessary. If possible, avoid tacking where you'll be quilting so you won't have to cut and remove tacks as you quilt. Remove the tacks with a scissors or tack-cutting tool after the quilting is completed.

**Tip**

Use white or off-white thread. That way, if a piece of it breaks off between your quilt layers it won't show through your quilt.

## 9

If you don't want to invest in hundreds of safety pins or a quilt basting gun, you can use traditional thread basting, but it's best to save this method for quilts where you'll mainly be quilting in the ditch.

Thread a milliner's needle with as long a thread as you can manage. Tie a large knot in one end. **Start at the center of the quilt and sew large stitches through all layers in a line to the top edge of the quilt.** Backstitch. Sew a second line of large stitches from the center to the bottom edge of the quilt, and backstitch. Repeat, sewing a line from the center to each side.

## 10

**Working within the quarter sections you have basted, sew lines horizontally and vertically every 6 inches.** Always work from the center lines out to the very edges of the quilt top so that the entire quilt is gridded into 6-inch squares. Try to place basting in areas you won't be quilting, as thread can be difficult to remove when stitched over numerous times. Basting can be removed after the quilting is completed or as sections are done.

# The Quilter's
# Problem Solver

## Basting & Batting Woes

| Problem | Solution |
|---------|----------|
| **Polyester batting is too wrinkled when it comes out of bag.** | Take the batting out of the bag several hours before you need it. Throw it in the dryer with a damp washcloth and on low heat. If necessary, tape or clamp the batting down along with the backing fabric while you baste. |
| **Batting shreds or is attacked by pets while you are quilting.** | As soon as you have basted the quilt layers, roll the edges of the backing and batting and safety pin them to the quilt top so all batting edges are safely enclosed in fabric. |
| **Thread basting gets caught on the presser foot.** | If the thread is not easily removed from the foot, clip it and it will come off immediately. Don't remove the thread, just leave the ends until quilting is completed and all basting is removed. |
| **Tacks from quilt basting tool leave holes in the fabric.** | Scratch your fingernail over the holes to bring the fibers back together. Or, rinse and machine dry the quilt after it is completed. |

## Skill Builder

### Save your back with these basting tips.

Whether crawling around the quilt on the floor or reaching over long tables, basting can be time-consuming and back-breaking work. Try one of these suggestions to make the work easier and faster.

❏ Trade basting sessions with a friend—she helps you and vice versa. It's more fun and the work goes twice as fast!

❏ Use a narrower table. Instead of having the entire quilt on one or two wide tables, baste in sections on a narrow table. The less you have to reach to baste, the happier your back will be.

## Try This!

**Buy the largest sizes of batting** so you can prewash or fluff the batting once and be ready for several projects. Keep leftover pieces of batting in a safe place with the sizes marked so you can grab the right one without unfolding all of the pieces.

# Selecting & Fitting
## *Quilting Designs*

The moment of truth comes when the quilt top is all pieced and pressed and you are left staring at a great expanse of empty space in which to quilt. Don't panic—this is the fun part! As soon as batting and backing are added the quilt takes on a new, more inviting appearance. The quilting can simply hold the layers of the quilt sandwich together or it can add a whole new dimension to the overall design. Quilting teacher and stencil designer Holice Turnbow provides guidelines for choosing designs and adjusting them to fit your quilt spaces.

## Getting Ready

When selecting designs for your quilt, it is helpful to think about a few things:

• How will your quilt be used? Every day use with lots of washing, or infrequently, with minimal wear and tear?

• What look do you want your quilt to have? Do you want the quilting to be an integral and important part of the total design, or is its main purpose utilitarian— to simply hold the layers together?

Your answers will help you decide on appropriate quilting designs. Also consider that quilting designs for machine quilting are different than those used in hand quilting. Motifs are less complex, with fewer starting and stopping points within the design. If you have a supply of hand-quilting stencils, you may be able to adapt them for machine quilting, as discussed on pages 58-61, or you have a choice of hundreds of continuous-line motifs designed specifically for machine quilting.

## What You'll Need

**Quilt top ready to be marked**

**Quilting designs (stencils or printed patterns)**

**Stencil-making materials:**

   **Plastic**

   **Permanent marking pen**

   **X-Acto knife**

**Fabric marking pencils**

**Copy machine (optional)**

**Pencil and tracing paper or vellum**

## Selecting & Fitting Quilting Designs

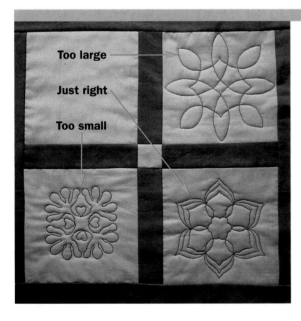

Too large

Just right

Too small

Quilting should fill the space without looking either sparse or crowded. The same is true of the details within the design. Heavy and close quilting within a design will add dimension to a quilt, but it may also be out of character with the style of the block or quilt.

Conversely, too little quilting gives the impression of too much space. **An easy rule to follow in choosing the overall size of a motif is to allow ¼ to 1 inch between the quilt design and the seam allowance in the blocks.** The bigger the block, the bigger the allowance. For example, a ¼-inch allowance on a 6-inch block will look quite different than on a 14-inch block.

If you have a design that you like that's compatible with your quilt design but it's either too large or too small, you can alter the size to fit your quilt. **The easiest way to change the size of a printed pattern is to enlarge or reduce it on a photocopy machine.** Simply select the percentage size difference you want, and print out a new size pattern. For instance, if you have a 6-inch design and want it to be 8 inches, you need to enlarge your original design to 133 percent (8 inches is 2 inches (or one-third) larger than 6 inches).

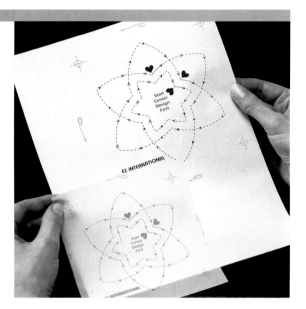

If your original design is a stencil, obviously you can't enlarge it on the photocopy machine. **However, you can make a drawing of the design through the stencil and enlarge that.** You can then use the printed pattern as your design to either trace from under the quilt with a light box or make a new stencil from the copy using Mylar and an X-Acto knife. See page 35 for guidance on making your own stencils.

If you don't have access to a photocopy machine or it doesn't suit your needs, you can enlarge or reduce your pattern by making some manual adjustments. For instance, you can enlarge your design by adding a row of outlining ½ inch outside the original design. This increases your overall design by 1 inch. **Or, you can add a new motif to the outer edges.** In this case, the overall size is increased by 2 inches by adding leaves to the corners of the floral design.

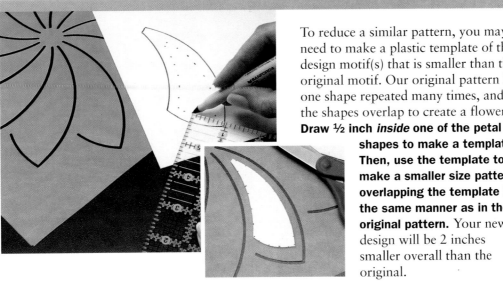

To reduce a similar pattern, you may need to make a plastic template of the design motif(s) that is smaller than the original motif. Our original pattern has one shape repeated many times, and the shapes overlap to create a flower. **Draw ½ inch *inside* one of the petal shapes to make a template. Then, use the template to make a smaller size pattern, overlapping the template in the same manner as in the original pattern.** Your new design will be 2 inches smaller overall than the original.

**Tip**

Modify a motif by more or less than 2" by tracing the template closer or farther away from the original design lines.

Alternate blocks or setting squares are a good place to use quilting to enhance the appearance of the quilt. Size, scale, balance, and compatibility are very important in making the right design selection. **In some cases, a repetition of the patchwork or appliqué design in the setting square adds continuity to the quilt design.** In our example, repeating the Dresden Plate shape is an easy way to achieve compatibility between the appliqué and the alternate setting blocks. Adding a background grid behind both appliqué and quilting designs would further unify the quilt surface.

**Borrowing from hand-quilting, one of the simplest patterns for quilting pieced blocks is to outline quilt or quilt in the ditch.** Quilting in the ditch and ¼-inch outlining require no marking because the seam line provides the guide for quilting. Quilting in the ditch (shown on right) adds dimension to the quilt without adding design elements. Quarter-inch outlining (shown on left), on the other hand, adds a secondary pattern to the quilt. See page 73 for more details on quilting in the ditch.

**Tip**

Quilting in the ditch is quicker and easier by machine than ¼" outline quilting. There's much less starting and stopping.

S E L E C T I N G & F I T T I N G D E S I G N S

8

You can add more definition and design to patchwork blocks by quilting a complementary design. The type of design you choose depends on the look or the effect you want to achieve. **Use a quilting stencil to add curves and movement to an angular block. Use free-motion meandering for no-mark quilting. Or use an overall cross-hatching—a safe choice that produces an antique look.**

## Fitting Border Designs

*Tip*

Sampler quilts especially benefit from unified quilting motifs, where there is so much variety already in the patchwork shapes and angles.

1

**When selecting a border or sashing design, look for a design that coordinates with the block design or that at least has some common elements or motifs.** By quilting the same curves or angles, you'll create a unified effect. **In addition to fitting the style of your quilting, the border design should fit the width of the border.** That way, you'll only need to adjust the design to fit the length of your particular quilt. Border patterns are sized according to the height of the design, with only enough repeats to give a complete design (plus perhaps the corner).

2

Regardless of the design, plan the corners of the borders carefully. The design should turn the corner gracefully or end in a logical manner. **Mark the corners first, then determine how to make the rest of the pattern repeat neatly.** You may need to either stretch out or shrink some sections of the border design to make it fit, but this won't be as noticeable as an interrupted corner would be.

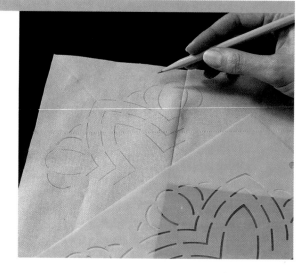

**To determine the amount of adjustment needed in the border design, cut paper the size of the border area and fold it in half lengthwise.** (You may need to tape sheets of paper together, or use vellum or tracing paper on a roll.) If your borders are particularly long (bed-size), fold the paper in half again. The fold marks will indicate your midpoint and quarter points.

Trace the design onto the paper, starting with the corner and moving along to the midpoint. If either the center point or the end point of the individual design unit aligns with the midpoint or quarter point of your border, the border design will fit without any adjustments.

**However, if this is not the case, measure the distance from the mid- or quarter-point of the border to the center or end point of the motif. This distance is the total amount of adjustment you need to make.**

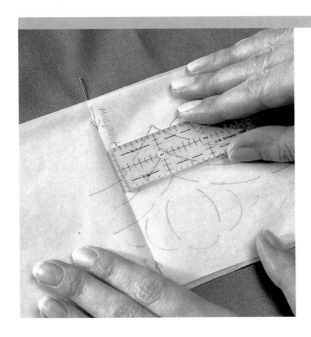

**Divide the amount of the adjustment by the number of motifs between the corner and the mid- or quarter-point (whichever point you measured to).** For instance, if your motif extended beyond the midpoint by 2 inches and you have 4 motifs that fit between the corner and the midpoint, then divide the 2-inch adjustment by 4. In this case, subtract ½ inch from each motif to make your border fit.

On the other hand, if a motif doesn't quite reach the midpoint, divide the amount that is *short* by the number of motifs from the corner to the midpoint and *add* your result to each motif to extend the border to fit.

SELECTING & FITTING DESIGNS

**6**

Redraw the shape of your motif on paper first (either extended or squished), to avoid mistakes when marking your quilt. **Cut the drawn design apart and slide the pieces either apart or closer together, as needed. Tape them in place.** With another sheet of tracing paper on top, trace the new shape of the design.

*Tip*

If you don't want to fuss with altering a border design, fill the gap at the mid-point where the designs don't meet with a flourish or other complementary design.

**7**

*Tip*

To emphasize marked quilting designs in a border, consider using filler quilting around them, such as stippling or cross-hatching.

If you're using a border stencil or pattern than does not provide a border corner, you can create one easily. **If you're working with a continuous border design, create an end point in the design by closing off the design and removing any extraneous lines.** This point will be the end of one border. **To mark the adjacent border, simply flip the design over, as shown, to create a mirror image.** The point where the two designs meet should be along the miter line of the border corner.

**8**

Some border designs are directional and must be reversed in order to retain a balance in the design at the corners. The most common place to make the reversal is at the midpoint of each border. **As with creating a corner design in Step 7 above, you can reverse the design at the midpoint by flopping your stencil or printed pattern to trace a mirror image.** By reversing a design at the midpoint, you give yourself some leeway for adjusting spacing, too. **Add a flourish to elongate the design, if needed.**

# The Quilter's
# Problem Solver

## Complementary Block & Border Designs

| Problem | Solution |
|---|---|
| **No border stencil to match block stencil.** | A border design doesn't have to perfectly match a block design or be purchased as a set to work. Try using part of the block design and modifying it to become a border design. Perhaps just a corner motif from the block design can be used to create a border by tracing it, then flopping it and tracing it in the opposite direction. Continue repeating this to create an undulating effect. The border design will convey a feel similar to the blocks, yet your design will be unique to your quilt. |
| **Border stencil is available, but not in the right size for the border.** | Again, there's no rule that says you must use a matching border design. But, if you're set on using that design, purchase the stencil and draw the design on paper. Then use a copy machine to enlarge or reduce it to fit the depth of your border. Now you can follow the step-by-step directions for fitting the length of the border to fit your quilt. Since you can't use the stencil to mark the quilt, try the needle punched method (see page 36), or use a light box to trace your drawn design. |

**Skill Builder**

### Plan ahead for a beautiful quilt.

❏ Coordinate motifs from one area of the quilt to another. Look for common shapes or motifs in each design to assure compatibility between quilting in blocks, setting triangles, sashings, and borders.

❏ Draw stencil motifs on paper first to be sure they fit the area and will fit your skill level. Some designs look more complicated than they are.

❏ If buying quilting stencils, take the quilt top along when you shop. It will be easier to select the right size, and the right style of design, too.

## Try This!

**Selecting a contrasting motif from a patchwork design often adds interesting effects to a quilt.** Instead of outline quilting a Log Cabin quilt, for instance, do something unexpected like a spiral, concentric circles, or a spider web. Save outline quilting for hand quilting, where it makes sense to avoid stitching over all the seam allowances. With your machine, quilting over seams isn't a problem. Surprise the viewer by choosing an unexpected motif that enhances the patchwork pattern with a bit of extra interest and fun.

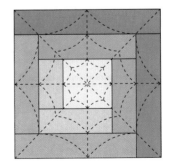

# Adapting Designs for
## *Continuous-Line Quilting*

**M**achine quilting and hand quilting have their similarities—after all, they are both done to hold the layers of the quilt together. But while it's commonplace to start and stop often when hand quilting (to move the hoop, to cut a new thread, or to move to a new design), machine quilters face fewer of these kinds of interruptions. To take advantage of this, it makes sense to use designs that can be stitched from start to finish without snipping the thread and starting over. Many patterns can be adapted to this kind of stitching, called continuous-line quilting. Sometimes all it takes is looking at designs with a fresh eye.

# Getting Ready

A continuous-line design offers several very significant advantages for machine quilters. You avoid repeated starting and stopping, which can be noticeable and distracting and which can also slow down the quilting process tremendously. In many cases, you also avoid the need to double over a previously stitched line—something that hand quilters avoid by passing the needle through the batting to travel to the beginning of another line.

How do you know if a design can be stitched continuously or not? If you have stencils or books of quilting designs for hand quilting, gather them together so you can analyze them by following the steps in this chapter. With a little effort, you'll probably be able to modify many of the designs you already have, and even develop some continuous-line patterns of your own. Then file the designs that seem suitable for continuous-line work together so they'll be handy for your next machine-quilting project.

## What You'll Need

**Quilting stencils**

**Books or magazines with quilting designs**

**Drawing paper**

**Sewing machine**

**Mechanical pencil**

**Eraser**

**Tracing paper, lightweight interfacing, or vellum**

**Masking or transparent tape**

**Ruler**

**Copy machine (optional)**

**Light box (optional)**

## Adapting Quilt Designs

**If you have patterns that were intended for hand quilting, you may be able to adapt them for continuous-line machine quilting.** Designs that have lots of lines going in different directions can't easily be adapted, but patterns for enclosed shapes, such as hearts and flowers, often can be modified.

**Draw the patterns on paper and connect the lines where the stencil had bridges.** Now trace around the design again, without lifting your pencil or doubling back over any lines. If you can't do this, you'll need to adapt the pattern.

Some patterns can be adapted by connecting one or more of the original lines, or by deleting some lines, as in our flower stencil example. **By deleting the short interior lines that connected the upper portion of the flower to the lower portion, the design can be stitched in one continuous line.**

Other designs merely need to be stitched in a different order than normally expected. For instance, a border of hearts would seem to require starting and stopping with each new heart. **But, by stitching across the tops only, then turning at the end and stitching the points you can start and stop only once.**

**If your pattern has elements that are unconnected from one another, use your imagination to connect them in a graceful, flowing way.** For instance, connect flowers with stems or vines, elongate hearts so they come together in a circle or overlap, connect cable lines so they are continuous instead of looking woven.

Once you've determined that your design will work for continuous stitching, try drawing it several times on paper, each time drawing in different sequences to discover the best way to quilt it. **Add arrows along the lines to help keep you on the right track.** When you start to quilt you will be familiar with the pattern and will be able to concentrate on the stitching rather than worrying about which way to stitch next.

A D A P T I N G  D E S I G N S

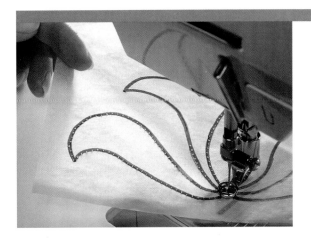

**5**

**Another way to see whether a quilting design will quilt easily is to draw the pattern on paper and sew it without thread.** This technique will familiarize you with the sequence of stitching as tracing did in Step 4, but stitching has an added benefit, too. This stitch test lets you check your stitch length and accuracy in following the lines before you mark and stitch your quilt.

If your hands want to quilt differently from the marked design, add lines to the design to accommodate that tendency.

**6**

Another way to create a continuous-line design is to trace or use a copy machine to make several copies of individual quilting motifs. **Place the copies next to each other or overlapping in a line or circle. Once you have arranged a design you like, tape the motifs together and trace them onto tissue paper or vellum, eliminating extraneous lines as you trace.** Use a window or light box so you can see the overlapping lines better for this step.

This method is also helpful when planning the corner quilting designs for the borders.

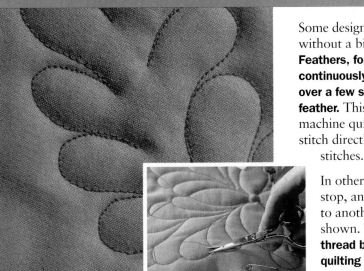

**7**

Some designs simply can't be adapted without a bit of duplicate stitching. **Feathers, for example, can be stitched continuously, but only if you backtrack over a few stitches to get to the next feather.** This is perfectly acceptable in machine quilting. Just take care to stitch directly over the first set of stitches.

In other cases, you may need to stop, anchor stitches, and move to another area of the design, as shown. **You don't need to clip your thread between sections until all quilting is completed.**

For more details on stitching feathers, see page 92. For stopping and starting, see page 68.

A D A P T I N G   D E S I G N S

# Handling a
# *Big Quilt*

I f you've ever wondered how to maneuver a queen- or king-size quilt, all puffy with
basted-in batting, under the arm of a home sewing machine, this chapter is for you!
While a huge industrial quilting machine with a long arm might seem to be the solution,
that's not a practical option for most quilters. Susan Stein shares two methods and
professional pointers for folding, rolling, scrunching, and smoothing the layers of a large quilt
so you can easily cope with the bulk at your own sewing machine.

# Getting Ready

Choose a low-loft batting for a large project so it will be lightweight and easy to compress into a small space. Baste the layers securely, because you will be manipulating the quilt over and over, unlike the hand-quilting process where you hold the layers in a hoop or frame and move the quilt less.

This chapter includes two methods of handling a large quilt. The Quilting a Grid method below is great if your quilt is arranged in rows of blocks. If not, or if your quilt is very large, see the alternate Quilting in Thirds method on page 66—*before* you baste your quilt. This technique reduces the bulk of the quilt sandwich tremendously, yet lets you have a whole-cloth backing unlike usual quilt-as-you-go methods.

 *The following chapters will be helpful in answering questions about getting ready to machine quilt a big quilt: "The Basics of Batting" on page 38, "Layering and Basting for Machine Quilting" on page 44, and "Setting Up a Machine-Quilting Workspace" on page 14.*

## What You'll Need

- **Office clamps or large rubber bands**
- **Large work surface**
- **Sewing Machine**
- **Kitchen timer**
- **Thread snips or embroidery scissors**
- **Rubber fingers, *or* leather/latex gloves, *or* Quilt Sew Easy hoop**
- **Comfortable chair (see page 17)**
- **Good lighting**
- **Container for safety pins**
- **Spare machine needles**
- **Milliner's needle and white thread**
- **Thread and extra prewound bobbin**

# Quilting a Grid

In the grid method, a quilt is first divided into quadrants by stitching in the ditch between the vertical and horizontal center rows of blocks. To prepare a large quilt for the first line of quilting, **accordion pleat the quilt layers to the right of the center line you'll be stitching so that they fit in the opening of your machine. Hold the pleats in place with office clamps or large rubber bands.** Some quilters roll rather than pleat the right side of the quilt, but it is harder to custom fit the roll to the size of the opening in your machine.

## Tip

Let the left side of the quilt lie flat on the sewing table and relax so it doesn't get too wrinkled or compressed.

**Tip**

When starting a new quilting session, warm up on a small wallhanging or practice quilt sandwich.

**Sit down at the machine, get comfortable, and arrange the pleated or rolled right side of the quilt in your lap or over your shoulder.** Either position should allow the quilt to freely enter the sewing machine with no drag. If the quilt drags, maneuvering it becomes difficult at best, and stitches will be uneven. The part of the quilt that has passed through the machine should be supported so that its weight does not pull against the needle from the back.

If your machine isn't built into a cabinet, a Plexiglas sewing table extension, as shown on page 12, is helpful.

**Tip**

Take breaks to rest your eyes, shoulders, back, arms, and hands. Set a kitchen timer to remind you to get up and stretch every half-hour.

If your quilt has blocks arranged in rows, quilt in the ditch along the center seam line or lattice strip using a walking foot or dual-feed mechanism. **Quilt both vertically and horizontally, beginning and ending at the first border.** This technique quarters the quilt surface, preventing any major shifting problems among the layers.

**Tip**

Quilt the borders next so you can bind the edges and protect the batting before doing detail quilting!

**Next, quilt in the ditch of the first border so that all subsequent quilting lines will not bulge out the edges of the borders.** Continue to quilt in the ditch along the rest of the seam lines between the lattice or blocks so that the whole quilt is stabilized for the detail quilting within the blocks. Reroll or pleat the quilt each time you change direction.

**To do the detail quilting, make a nest for your hands that opens up the maximum work area around the needle.** It is necessary to have as much flat space to work in as possible so there will be no drag on the quilt—especially for free-motion quilting. If you pleat a large quilt, it will be a lot easier to open up the folds in the area you want to quilt than if it would be if you rolled the quilt.

When you need to reposition your hands, leave the needle down in the fabric until your hands are back in position. When you need to reposition the quilt so you can do detail quilting in the next area, leave the bobbin threads connected. **Raise the needle, move to the new area, and after taking a few small stitches or stitching in place, simply clip the top thread and leave the bottom thread intact.**

Because you aren't continually stopping to remove the quilt from the machine to clip the bobbin thread, you won't have to maneuver your quilt quite so much. This saves wear and tear on both you and the quilt layers!

*Tip*

You can leave the top threads connected too, unless they'll be in the way of your next quilting path.

When your kitchen timer goes off and you return from your scheduled break, **turn the quilt over and clip all of the long bobbin threads that connect one quilting area to another.** Because you're clipping the threads while looking at the back instead of doing it blindly trying to find the bobbin thread under a mass of layers, you'll be less likely to clip a hole in the quilt back while snipping threads.

*Tip*

During breaks, hang the quilt on the design wall. You can evaluate your progress while the quilt layers get to relax and breathe.

HANDLING A BIG QUILT

# Quilting in Thirds

**Tip**

Mark the left and right batting sections after cutting them apart from the center panel so you'll remember which piece fits where.

## 1

For a very large quilt or one that's not arranged in rows of blocks, use Debra Wagner's technique of quilting in thirds. **Cut the batting into thirds and baste the center one-third piece into the center of the quilt.** (Note: Only the batting is cut into thirds, not the backing or quilt top!) The outer thirds of the quilt will be very light, flexible, and easy to maneuver since they contain no batting.

## 2

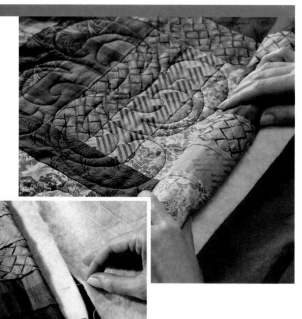

**Quilt the middle third of the quilt, ending all stitching about 2 inches away from the edges of the batting.** If you quilt too close to the edge of the batting, it will be harder to whip-stitch the batting together without catching either the quilt top or backing in those stitches.

Then insert the second piece of batting between the backing and quilt top. **Firmly stitch the butted edges of the batting together by hand with a whipstitch,** and then baste the three quilt layers together. See page 46 in "Layering and Basting for Machine Quilting" for details on hand stitching batting panels together.

## 3

**Quilt the newly basted section, making sure that quilting merges and blends with the previous quilting.** You don't want a vertical line to appear where there is little or no quilting. Plus, quilting over the batting seam will hold the batting securely in place. Repeat, joining the batting and quilting for the last third of the quilt.

# The Quilter's
# Problem Solver

## Getting a Quilt to Lie Flat

| Problem | Solution |
|---|---|
| **Quilt patches are wrinkled from being scrunched to fit under the sewing machine arm.** | Place the quilt on the floor or design wall and mist it with cold water. Let it dry completely before moving it and the wrinkles will be gone. |
| **Quilt does not lie flat after the quilting is completed.** | Place the quilt on the floor or design wall and use a steamer or steam iron to shrink out the fullness. Don't touch the quilt with the iron or steamer, but get very close so steam will have maximum impact. This technique works best on cotton/poly or cotton batting. Use caution with 100 percent polyester batting—it can melt. Let the quilt dry completely before moving it. |

**Skill Builder**

### Lighten the load of a big quilt with these tips.

❏ If you have pin basted, remove pins after quilting a grid to lessen the weight of the quilt and reduce the chance of snagging a pin on your machine. Pin again only in the area that you are working on.

❏ Make sure the machine and table surfaces are very slippery. Leave the needle down when you reposition your hands so the quilt does not slip out of position, but be careful not to pull on the needle and bend it.

❏ Even on slippery surfaces, the weight of a large quilt can cause drag. Try rubber fingers, leather or latex gloves, or the Quilt Sew Easy machine quilting hoops to get a better grip on the quilt.

## Try This!

**Here's some advice for dealing with tucks on the quilt back.** It has happened to everyone at some time—when you're clipping thread tails, you find a tuck on the back of the quilt. The first reaction is to be annoyed, but remember, unless you're entering a competition, no one is giving you a grade on your quilt. A couple of tucks on the back of the quilt are insignificant. Focus on the positive. You are completing a large quilt in your lifetime!

However, if the tuck still bothers you, remove several inches of stitching on either side of it. Ease out the excess fabric and thread baste in place. Now you can restitch the line from the front of the quilt, confident that you won't be requilting a pucker on the back.

HANDLING A BIG QUILT

# Learning How to
## Start & Stop

**J**ust like when you were learning to drive a car, knowing how to start and stop are two of the most important skills you can master in machine quilting (not to mention the ones you'll use most frequently). You have a variety of choices of how to go about knotting off your threads. The method you choose may be based on the style of quilting you'll be doing, so try each method and you'll be ready to tackle any technique.

## Getting Ready

For this and the lessons that follow, it's best to practice before starting out on a real live quilt. So, make a practice quilt sandwich using two 14-inch squares of muslin or solid color cotton fabric with a 14-inch square of batting in the middle. Place the backing fabric on a flat surface and lay the square of batting on top of it. Smooth the top fabric over the batting. Pin baste the three layers together with safety pins (rust-proof) at 3- to 4-inch intervals, or use a quilt basting gun, if you prefer.

You can use this lesson as a chance to test different materials, such as different varieties of thread, different brands or lofts of batting, and so on. To do so, make several practice sandwiches and write on them which kind of thread and batting you used for future reference.

### What You'll Need

**Practice quilt sandwich**

**Nickel-plated safety pins, *or* quilt basting gun**

**Sewing machine**

**Walking foot or darning foot**

**Machine-quilting needle**

**Thread and extra prewound bobbin**

**Thread snips or embroidery scissors**

## Knots

Knots can be used for either machine-guided or free-motion quilting. The knots are formed by having the needle move up and down in place while the fabric is stationary. Attach either your walking foot or darning foot, depending upon whether you'll be doing machine-guided or free-motion quilting.

**With the presser foot raised, move the fly wheel slowly, take one stitch, and pull up a loop of the bobbin thread to the top of the fabric.** Note: This step is necessary for every method of starting machine quilting. Leaving the bobbin thread under the fabric can result in tangles on the quilt back.

Knotting is a good method to use if your quilt has a printed backing fabric because the busyness of the print hides the knot.

**Tip**

More isn't always better. Don't take too many stitches or your knots will be visible.

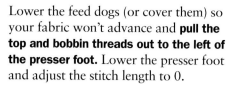

Lower the feed dogs (or cover them) so your fabric won't advance and **pull the top and bobbin threads out to the left of the presser foot.** Lower the presser foot and adjust the stitch length to 0.

**Insert the needle back into the fabric at the same point where the bobbin thread came up.** Take three or four stitches in a stationary position to anchor them securely. **A small knot will form on the back of the quilt sandwich.**

For machine-guided quilting, raise the feed dogs and set the stitch length at about 10 stitches per inch. For free-motion quilting, leave the feed dogs lowered.

The knots are tiny, so take care not to clip them from the quilt.

When you've completed stitching a row or a design, stop with the needle in the fabric. Repeat the knotting process described for starting. (Remember to lower the feed dogs if you're doing machine-guided quilting, and set the stitch length to 0.) Take a few stitches in place.

Lift the presser foot and remove the quilt. **Clip the top thread close to the fabric,** then turn to clip the bobbin thread. Clip the starting threads close to the fabric, too.

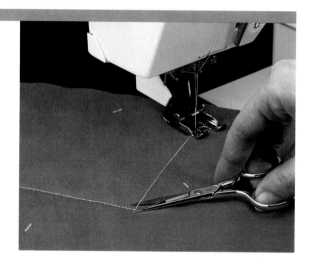

## Short Stitches

For free-motion quilting, you don't need to adjust stitch length. Simply move the quilt sandwich more quickly to lengthen stitches.

Short stitches are a very secure way to anchor machine quilting. The stitches are so small that they are difficult to remove (even with a seam ripper!), and they're practically invisible.

Insert the needle and pull up the bobbin thread, as in Step 1 on page 69. Set the stitch length to 20 stitches per inch (about .5 on a 0–5 scale setting). Lower the presser foot, hold the threads, and take a few stitches. **Let go of the threads and gradually increase the stitch length to about 10 stitches per inch while you continue to sew.**

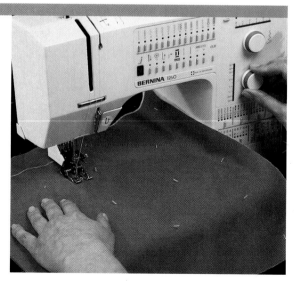

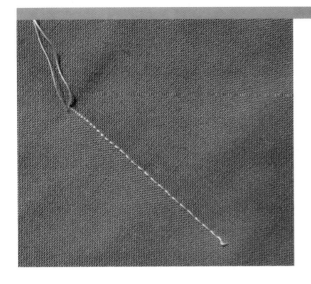

Stop stitching ¼ to ½ inch before you want to end your stitching line. **For machine-guided stitching, use your right hand to gradually adjust the stitch length from 10 down to 20 stitches per inch as you continue to sew.** Take four more stitches to end.

For free-motion stitching, slow the speed at which you move the quilt so the stitches begin to get shorter. Take about four very short stitches and stop. Remove the quilt sandwich and clip threads close to the fabric.

*Tip*

After taking three short stitches, take one longer one. A small loop of bobbin thread will pull to the top. Snip it instead of flipping over your whole quilt.

## Burying Thread Tails

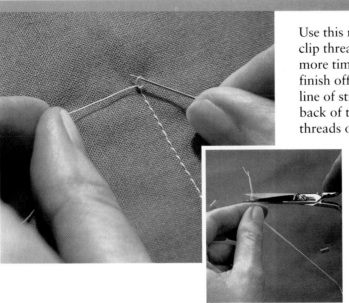

Use this method if you prefer not to clip threads close to the quilt top. It's more time consuming, but will let you finish off the beginning and end of each line of stitching without a knot on the back of the quilt or blunt ends of threads on the top.

Begin and end stitching with normal stitch length settings. Leave thread tails at least 3 inches long. **Pull gently on the top or bobbin thread to pull both threads to the same side of the quilt. Hold the threads together and trim the ends so both threads are 3 inches long.**

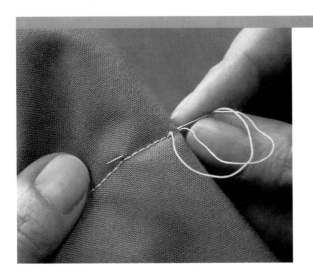

Thread a sharp, large-eyed needle with both threads. **Insert the needle into the quilting stitch at the end of the stitching line, guiding it into the batting layer for 1 or 2 inches along the line of stitches. Bring the needle out through the top layer of fabric** and clip the threads close to the fabric. Repeat for each starting and stopping point.

*Tip*

Smooth the fabric and the tiny ends of threads will disappear into the quilt layers.

# Machine-Guided
## *Straight-Line Quilting*

S nap on a walking foot, raise the feed dogs, and you're off! Machine-guided quilting is
perfect for quilting in the ditch as well as for channel quilting, cross-hatching, diagonal
line quilting, and more. These types of designs make great filler quilting and look
especially nice surrounding appliqué motifs. Machine-guided quilting is quite easy to do, since
your sewing machine is doing the work of moving the quilt layers evenly and consistently
under the needle. The result is precision stitching—no puckers, wrinkles, or creases!

## Getting Ready

A walking foot or dual-feed mechanism moves quilt layers through the machine at exactly the same pace, leaving little room for layers to shift and pucker. Make sure you know how to properly attach your machine's walking foot (if you don't have one, see your machine dealer) or engage the built-in even-feed system (on Pfaffs only).

Feed dogs need to be engaged, so check your manual if you are uncertain how to raise and lower them. Set your stitch length for a bit longer than normal, insert a new needle, and you're ready to start quilting.

*Since machine-guided quilting usually involves more stopping and starting than free-motion quilting, you may find it helpful to refer to "Learning How to Start and Stop" on page 68.*

"Learning How to Start and Stop" on page 68.

### What You'll Need

- **Sewing machine**
- **Spare machine needles**
- **Layered and basted quilt top or practice quilt sandwich**
- **Walking foot**
- **Rotary cutting ruler**
- **Hera or quilt marking pencil**
- **Thread and extra prewound bobbin**
- **Nickel-plated safety pins, *or* quilt basting gun**
- **Guide for walking foot (optional)**
- **Twin needle, size 6.0 or 8.0 (optional)**

## Quilting in the Ditch

The most basic type of machine-guided quilting is stitching in the ditch. The ditch is the seam line between any patchwork pieces, whether it's the seam between blocks and sashing or between pieces within a block.

In-the-ditch quilting gives you a built-in stitching line—there's no need to mark. You can quilt a quilt entirely with in-the-ditch quilting, or you can supplement the technique with other forms of machine quilting.

**Lower the machine needle into one of the seams, anchor the stitches, and stitch along the lower side of the seam line.** The lower side is the one that doesn't have the seam allowances pressed toward it.

**2**

When crossing a seam intersection, you may find that the lower side of the seam shifts to the opposite side of where you were stitching. **Simply shift your stitching so you are still following along whichever side of the seam is lower.** These slight shifts in stitching won't be noticeable, whereas continuing to stitch on the same side of the seam allowance would be. If you stitch through the side with the seam allowances, you may create a bulky ridge, which will be obvious. Also, you may encounter thread tension problems stitching through the bulk of the seam allowances.

# Cross-Hatching

**1**

*Tip*

For best visibility of lines marked with a hera, mark *after* layering and basting. The batting helps define the marked crease.

Unlike quilting in the ditch, cross-hatching needs to be marked. **Using a rotary-cutting ruler and either a hera or marking pencil, mark a line across the center of the quilt block or area you'll be quilting.** For a 1-inch grid, move the ruler 1 inch to the right and mark a second line. Continue marking parallel lines at 1-inch intervals across the quilt block. Turn the quilt sandwich 90 degrees and mark lines at 1-inch intervals in the same manner. Use one of the cross markings on your ruler to ensure that all lines are perpendicular to the first set of lines.

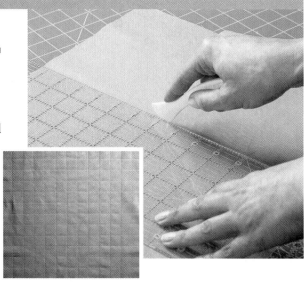

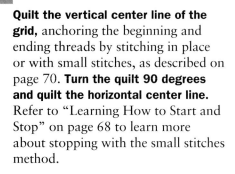

**2**

*Tip*

If your walking foot has a metal bar attachment, you can mark only the first line of the grid, then set this guide for a 1" interval.

**Quilt the vertical center line of the grid,** anchoring the beginning and ending threads by stitching in place or with small stitches, as described on page 70. **Turn the quilt 90 degrees and quilt the horizontal center line.** Refer to "Learning How to Start and Stop" on page 68 to learn more about stopping with the small stitches method.

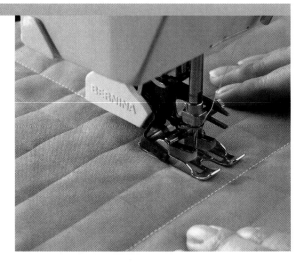

**After quilting the center line in each direction, quilt the outermost lines on all four sides of the quilt.** This stabilizes the entire surface, making it easy to quilt in any section of the block without creating puckers or distorting the fabric.

**Starting in any quadrant of the quilt, quilt the line that is midway between the center line and the outermost line of stitches.** Turn the quilt 90 degrees and repeat this step. Work around all four sides of the quilt in the same manner, turning it after each line of stitches. By working in this manner, you'll be able to ease any fullness in the fabric evenly over the entire quilt.

**When all lines have been stitched, your cross-hatched grid will be even and smooth, without any puckers in the fabric.**

Cross-hatching is often done diagonally across entire quilts, as a background filler for appliqué blocks or in unpieced alternate blocks in a patchwork quilt. Mark and stitch a diagonal grid in the same manner as described in Steps 1 through 4, however, mark the first line at a 45 degree angle to the edge of the quilt sandwich. **Align the 45 degree mark on the rotary cutting ruler with the edge of the fabric.** Mark lines on the opposite diagonal.

*Tip*

For another interesting look, try a diamond-shaped grid. Align the 60 degree marking on your ruler with the fabric edge.

**6**

If you prefer, outline stitch around the appliqué shapes before doing the cross-hatch quilting (see page 74). Then, starting at the edge of the appliqué block, quilt any one of the diagonal lines to within ⅜ inch of the first appliqué shape you encounter. **Adjust the stitch length to about 20 stitches per inch and continue quilting until you reach the outline quilting around the shape.**

**7**

Lift the presser foot and cross over the appliqué shape, pulling the threads gently. **Lower the presser foot on the other side of the appliqué shape and quilt a few short stitches on this side of the motif.** Then lengthen the stitch length to about 10 stitches per inch. Continue quilting on the marked line, crossing over each appliqué shape as you come to it.

**Quilt each of the remaining grid lines in the same manner to complete the block.** Clip the crossover threads close to the surface of the quilt sandwich when all quilting is completed.

**8**

Double cross-hatching is another pleasing effect. Simply stitch a grid as described above (either straight of grain or diagonal). **Then measure ¼ inch from the center line in one direction and mark another stitching line.** If your presser foot is ¼ inch wide, you may not need to mark the second set of lines. However, if you don't have a ¼-inch-wide walking foot, continue to mark a second set of lines ¼ inch away from the first set. **Stitch all lines in the same order as described in Steps 2 through 4.**

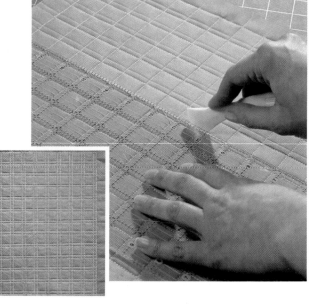

*Tip*

Make sure you are marking all the new lines consistently. Don't mark some to the right of a stitched line and others to the left.

# The Quilter's
# Problem Solver

## Starting, Stopping & Turning the Quilt

| Problem | Solution |
|---------|----------|
| **Stitching in the ditch seems relatively easy but involves turning the quilt a lot.** | True, you need to stop stitching at the end of each stitching line, and move onto the next row or line of stitching. Quite often, this involves stitching in a different direction, so the quilt must be turned. If the quilt is larger than a wallhanging, it pays to accordion-fold the quilt so it is easy to maneuver (see page 63). If your quilt is rolled to fit under the machine, you'll find it's too stiff and inflexible to turn or move easily. |
| **Cross-hatching looks nice but creates a lot of starting and stopping knots.** | If you don't like the look of knots or closely clipped threads, try this. Instead of taking three stitches in place and clipping the thread tail close to the quilt top, start each stitching line with short stitches instead. Then, don't clip the thread tail, but thread it onto a hand-sewing needle and use the needle to bury the thread tail between the quilt layers. No more knots! |

**STRAIGHT-LINE QUILTING**

### Skill Builder

**Use grid quilting to produce a variety of looks for different quilts.**

❏ Antique quilts typically have tiny grids, often spaced no more than ½ inch apart. Use mono-filament thread for stitching and an unwashed cotton batting in the quilt. Wash the quilt when completed to shrink the batting and you'll have an instant antique!

❏ Variegated rayons or metallic threads shimmer on the quilt surface, making them pop to the foreground instead of receding into the background. Use them to update cross-hatching from a classic to a contemporary look.

❏ Use a 6.0 or 8.0 twin needle for a quick and easy double cross-hatched grid. Your lines will be perfectly spaced, and you'll only have to mark one set of lines, not two.

### Try This!

There's no rule that says grid quilting has to be done with a straight stitch. **If your sewing machine has decorative stitches, try some of them for machine-guided quilting.** Try them on a practice quilt sandwich first, to see how you like their effects. Here's just one example: If you have a scallop stitch, you can make a clamshell grid. Measure the length of the scallop from point to point. That's how far apart you'll need to place your lines to have the scallops intersect to create the clamshell.

Scallop stitch

Clamshell grid

# Machine-Guided
## *Gentle Curves*

Designs like flowing cables, which have gently curved lines, are appropriate for machine-guided quilting techniques because you don't need to turn a quilt frequently to stitch them. This type of quilted curve adds a nice bit of counterpoint to angular patchwork, and best of all, it's easy to master. The walking foot and feed dogs help guide your quilt sandwich under the needle smoothly. With a little practice, you'll have no problem staying on the marked lines and producing even, consistent quilting stitches.

# Getting Ready

Choose curved designs for machine-guided quilting carefully. If curves are too deep, you'll have to stop frequently and lift your presser foot to turn the quilt. Shallow curves that undulate gently, such as a vine or cable design, are the best choices. A feathered wreath, on the other hand, should be saved for free-motion quilting.

For machine guided curves, attach your walking foot or engage the machine's dual-feed mechanism. Make sure the feed dogs are up, and you're ready to go.

**Sewing machine**

**Thread and extra prewound bobbin**

**Walking foot**

**Layered and basted quilt top or practice quilt sandwich**

**Quilt marking pencil**

**Quilting stencils with curved designs**

**Freezer paper or Con-Tact paper**

**Curved items for tracing (plate, quilter's flexicurve)**

**Craft scissors**

**Thread snips or embroidery scissors**

**Straight pins**

**Latex gloves (optional)**

# Gentle Curves

Decide whether or not you need to mark the curved lines on your quilt top. For an unpieced border or alternate block, you'll probably want to mark the designs. **You can mark curves directly on the quilt with a purchased stencil or cut them out of a stick-on paper such as freezer paper or Con-Tact paper and stitch around them.**

In addition to stencils, you can mark curved designs with other items, such as a saucer, dinner plate, or a quilter's flexicurve. See page 32 for different methods of quilt marking.

**2**

Once your quilt is marked and basted, you're ready to start stitching. **Gently push a little "speed bump" of fabric in front of the presser foot as you work.** This will keep the fabric relaxed, especially at the location of the needle, and help to guide the quilt through the machine smoothly. Too much finger tension in front of the needle will produce stitches that are too small, while pulling on the fabric from behind the presser foot will create long, uneven stitches.

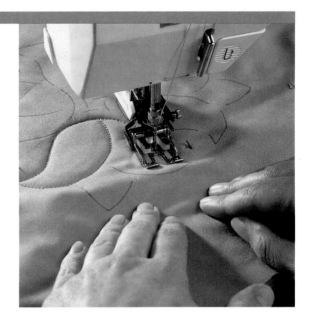

**Tip**

If you find it tricky to maneuver a quilt with your palms, slip on a pair of latex surgical gloves (available at pharmacies) for traction.

**3**

Because a sewing machine needle does not know that you want it to quilt curves, it's helpful to think in terms of "putting the fabric where the needle is." **This makes it easy to maneuver the long, shallow curves by simply using the palms of your hands to pivot the quilt sandwich gently, while you continue stitching.**

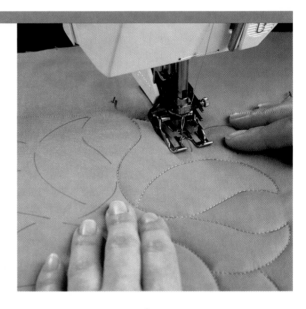

**Tip**

For smooth curves, stop and pivot at even intervals. For instance, pivot consistently after every three or after every four stitches.

**4**

For tighter curves, like those marked from a saucer's edge, use the sewing machine needle to help you pivot the quilt sandwich. **Whenever you need to change the position of the fabric in order to continue stitching on the marked line, stop, raise the presser foot, and move the quilt sandwich slightly so that the needle is in position to continue stitching.** Then lower the presser foot and take one or two more stitches. Repeat this process as necessary, remembering to keep the needle lowered whenever you raise the presser foot.

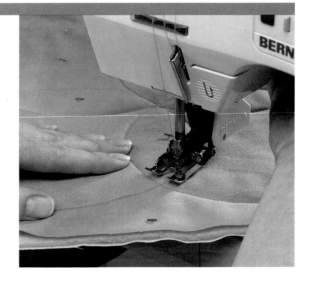

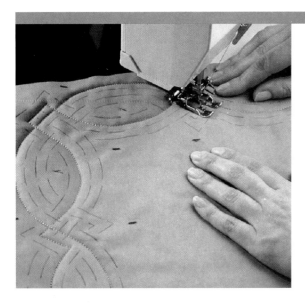

After stitching one line of a cable or other continuous design, move on to the next, working your way to the outer lines. **Check your stitching to see that your curves are smooth and even, with no angles or puckers.** Sew all lines of a cable or similar design in the same direction.

*Tip*

To correct a sharp angle, restitch the curve, overlapping some stitches for security, then gently remove the angled stitches.

Curved quilting lines don't have to be reserved for unpieced borders or alternate blocks. You can create a look of movement among patchwork blocks with traditional curved quilting patterns or more innovative, free-form designs.

If you choose to quilt curves over patchwork, you can mark a specific design or simply use the intersections of the patchwork pieces as starting and stopping points of a curve. **Stitching curved designs over patchwork seams is much easier by machine than by hand.**

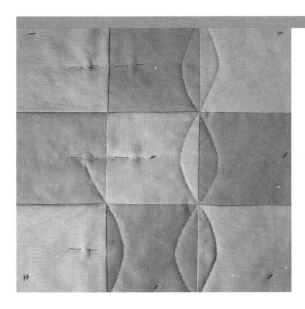

When quilting curved lines inside a patchwork shape, it is not always necessary to mark the lines on the quilt top first. **Simply determine how deep you want your curved line to be, and place a straight pin to mark that depth at the midpoint of the pieced shape.** As you stitch, make sure your line has a defined curve. Avoid stitching a very shallow curve, which can sometimes look like you were trying to stitch in the ditch and missed. When you reach the pin, remove it and continue stitching, taking care to match the second half of your curved line to the first.

M A C H I N E - G U I D E D   G E N T L E   C U R V E S

# Free-Motion
## *Quilting Basics*

*O*nce you've mastered the feel of machine-guided quilting, it won't be long until you're ready to move on to the wonderful world of free-motion quilting. Instead of being confined to straight lines (and a lot of stopping and turning your quilt), you can enjoy the freedom of stitching in any direction you desire, often for long, uninterrupted stretches of graceful quilting. From gentle meandering and delicate stippling to following any drawn design, your quilting will only be limited by your imagination.

# Getting Ready

Free-motion quilting can be done in many different ways, from meandering to stippling to echo quilting and more. There are two basic methods that you need to get comfortable with before exploring all the options and even inventing some new ones. One method is called meander quilting. This is totally free-motion quilting without a drawn or traced design—you move your quilt randomly under the needle. The second method is continuous-line quilting, where you move your quilt to follow a specific pattern drawn on the quilt top.

To do any type of free-motion quilting, you need to lower the feed dogs. If they can't be lowered on your machine, cover them by taping a business card or index card over them. Attach a darning foot to your machine and set your stitch length to zero. You determine the stitch length by how quickly you move your quilt under the needle while you sew, not by the stitch-length setting.

## Meander Quilting

If you've never done free-motion quilting before, it's helpful to start with a plan or an idea of a design you want to stitch before you start out on your actual quilt. **Draw a continuous line that wanders over an 8½ × 11-inch sheet of paper (not lifting your pencil ensures the continuous line).**

The line should be curvy and flowing, like a meandering brook or river. And, like a river, the line should not cross over itself at any point. **Start in one corner of the paper and let your pencil wander around until the sheet is filled.** Try not to have any sharp points, but rather make your line bend and twist with smooth curves.

Lower or cover the feed dogs and
attach the darning foot. **Without
thread, practice stitching along your
drawn line.** Don't turn the paper, but
rather move it forward, backward, or
from side to side to stay on the line.
Stop as needed to reposition your
hands so you can guide your paper.

**When you've stitched the
entire paper, hold it up to the
light to check your "stitches."**
If the holes are very close
together, you're moving your
quilt more slowly than you are
pressing on the foot pedal. If
your stitches are very long,
you're moving the quilt faster
than you are pressing on the
foot pedal.

Meander quilting is done exactly the
same way on fabric: with lowered
feed dogs, a stitch length of 0, and a
darning foot on the machine. Anchor
stitches (see page 69) and begin
moving your quilt. **Place your thumbs
and index fingers on either side of the
presser foot to hold the fabric taut
and smooth.** Guide the fabric
smoothly in S-shaped curves, moving
it at an even pace. Keep the needle
moving at a steady speed, too. If you
speed up the needle, your stitches will
become very short unless you also
speed up your hand movements.

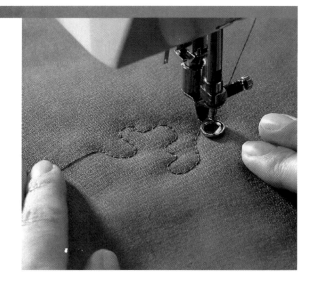

When you've filled in an area with
meander quilting and you're ready to
move to the next one, anchor your
stitches, raise the needle, and move to
the next area. **After stitching a curve
or two, you can clip the connecting
threads out of your way.**

Use meander quilting in a variety of places. **It makes a nice background filler in patchwork blocks, where the curving lines provide interesting counterpoint to the straight lines and angles of the geometric pieces.** Meandering is also often used as an all-over design, stitched completely across entire patchwork patterns. Meandering in the background of appliqué shapes also creates a pleasing effect.

*Tip*

Think of your stitching lines as exaggerated jigsaw puzzle shapes that meander in all directions.

## Continuous-Line Quilting

Continuous-line designs are stitched in the same manner as meandering, using a darning foot with the feed dogs lowered, but continuous-line designs aren't random. They follow a specific pattern. **So begin by marking your pattern on your quilt top.** See "Adapting Designs for Continuous-Line Quilting" on page 58 and "Marking Quilting Designs" on page 32.

*Tip*

A light box works great for tracing printed quilting patterns onto darker fabric that's difficult to see through.

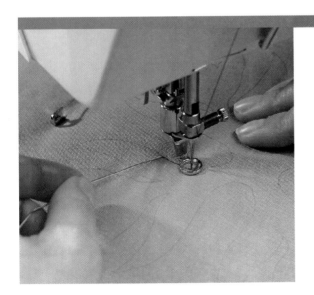

**Insert the needle at one of the starting points (many continuous-line patterns can be started anywhere), and anchor your stitches.** The short stitches method is a good anchoring method for continuous-line quilting since your starting and stopping points become nearly invisible on both the front and the back of the finished quilt. For more information on this method, see pages 68–71.

### 3

**Stitch along the marked lines of the design, moving the quilt so the needle stays on the drawn line.** You do not have to turn your quilt as a design curves or bends. Since the feed dogs are lowered, you have the freedom to move your quilt forward, backward, or from side to side to follow the design. **Continue stitching in the direction of the arrows on your design.**

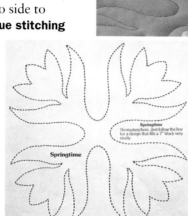

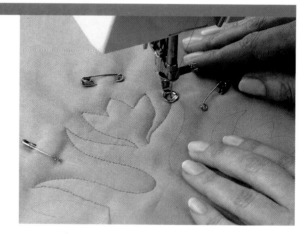

### 4

**When you come to a point in the marked design, pause with the needle in the fabric. Take one more stitch at the same point, then continue to stitch along the marked design.** This extra stitch will keep the points sharp and crisp, rather than rounded or squared off.

### 5

Continue stitching the rest of the design, and end with short stitches. Clip the thread tails close to the fabric. Stand back and admire your work!

# The Quilter's
# Problem Solver

## Stitches in the Wrong Place

| Problem | Solution |
|---------|----------|
| **Stitches veered off marked continuous-line design.** | Both of these problems have the same solution. Whether you're meandering or following a pattern, it's not uncommon to sometimes stitch where you didn't want to. When this happens, simply stop stitching, lift the presser foot to release the top tension, and slide the quilt back to where the needle is directly over the last bit of "correct" stitching before you drifted astray. Don't clip the thread. Take three or four tiny stitches on top of the last several correct stitches to secure them, then continue stitching with your regular stitch length. When you've stitched far enough past the mistake, stop with the needle down and use a seam ripper to go back and remove the errant stitches. |
| **Meandering extended beyond background and into patchwork.** | |

### Skill Builder

**Wear latex surgical gloves when you're free-motion quilting.**

The traction of the rubber and the snug fit of the gloves provide complete control while guiding your quilt. The added bonus is that you can rethread the needle, unclip safety pins, or do any other kind of detail work without having to take off the gloves. Plus, any dirt or oils on your hands won't transfer to the quilt.

## Try This!

**Create different looks by varying your stitches or patterns.**

❏ Try zigzag meandering by setting your stitch width to wider than 0. Just make certain your selected zigzag width isn't too wide for the needle to pass through the darning foot opening. The patterns you create will vary by how fast you move your needle and fabric.

❏ Instead of jigsaw puzzle shapes, try different ones, like loops, zigzags, or spirals. You can even follow a printed design in a fabric for inspiration. Experiment and have fun!

# Free-Motion
## *Stipple Quilting*

S tippling is one of the prize effects of machine quilting. Quilters who would never dream of stippling by hand find they can add this incredibly beautiful visual texture to a project in no time at all. Small, tightly spaced stippling is especially striking as a setting for appliqué shapes, quilted motifs, or trapunto designs. When stippling is done with larger shapes, it is commonly known as meander quilting, perhaps because the curved lines look like meandering streams.

## Getting Ready

You'll want to practice stippling before adding it to a quilt. Here are some things to keep in mind:

• Stippling and meandering are done by free-motion quilting.

• Stitch small and close. Move the quilt slowly so your stitch length is no more then ⅛ inch.

• Sew slowly. Let your hands guide the quilt underneath the presser foot.

• Plan a path. You don't want to get stuck with nowhere to go. Concentrate on an area approximately 2 × 2 inches, fill it, then move on to the next area.

• Practice until you find the right speed for both your foot on the pedal and your hands guiding the quilt.

> *Refer to "Learning How to Start and Stop" on page 68 to get your stipple quilting off to a great start.*

Refer to "Learning How to Start and Stop" on page 68 to get your stipple quilting off to a great start.

### What You'll Need

**Sewing machine**

**Darning foot or Big Foot**

**Basted and partially quilted quilt**

**100% cotton thread**

**Pencil and paper**

## Stipple Quilting

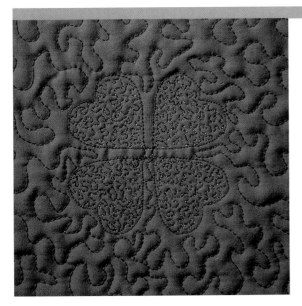

**When stippling, your lines of stitching should be about ⅛ to ¼ inch apart.** Meandering, on the other hand, is the correct term when the lines are spaced farther apart (see page 84). While the terms are often used interchangeably, the distinction does really exist. Stippling is used more for filling in small areas, such as inside quilted shapes or as a background for quilted or appliquéd designs. **Meander quilting is useful for filling in large areas, such as borders or around other quilted designs, and is sometimes used to quilt over entire quilt tops.** In both types of quilting, the stitching lines should not cross each other.

*Tip*

Practice drawing stippling in 3" squares with pencil and paper to quickly get the knack of leaving yourself an exit.

**2**

**To stipple inside a quilted motif, pin-baste or tack the areas of your quilt that are not already quilted.** Make sure to leave the area you will be stippling free of pins so you can maneuver your presser foot without catching it in a pin. **If the area is larger than about 3 × 3 inches, divide it visually into smaller areas that you will fill before moving into the next area. This makes it easier to stipple without getting "stuck" in a corner with nowhere to go.** Concentrate on one area at a time, as indicated in the boxed section at right.

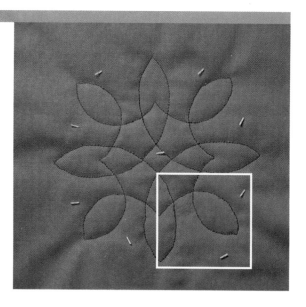

**3**

**Begin in a corner or at an edge of the area you'll be stippling.** Using short stitches, begin stitching directly on top of a line of stitches in the motif you are stippling around. This will make it hard to determine where you started quilting once the project is completed.

**4**

After anchoring your stitches, begin stippling, using your fingertips to guide the quilt toward yourself and to the left as you work, rather than allowing the fabric to move behind the needle. This keeps the stitches in front of the needle, where you can see them clearly.

As you stitch, imagine you are drawing small jigsaw puzzle-shaped pieces with your needle and thread. Move slowly enough that you can control the shape and size of your stitches. **Keep the puzzle-pieced shapes about ⅛ to ¼ inch apart, and vary their shapes and their directions.**

**When you are about three-quarters done stippling your first area, start looking for a way to complete the area and still leave an exit to move on to the next.** It's important to keep the line continuous, so plan accordingly.

**When you are finished stippling, end your stitching by joining the line of stitching to a previously stitched line, using very small stitches.** Trim the threads close to the surface of the quilt.

The secret to good stippling is to make the design look random. Keep your fingers relaxed and change directions every ¼" to ½".

**6**

**Stippled areas looks flatter than other quilted areas, which accentuates the puffiness of quilted motifs.** It also creates a rich, textured area for the light to play in, which adds visual interest. In the background of a trapuntoed design, such as the quilt shown on page 88, stippling serves this purpose very effectively. (See "The Basics of Machine Trapunto" on page 102.)

**7**

Because stippled areas are flatter than other areas of a quilt, you may see a ripple effect if the amount of quilting on a project isn't balanced. **For instance, if the interior of a quilt isn't heavily quilted but there's lots of stippling in the border, the edges of the quilt will tend to ripple.**

To avoid this situation, plan quilting designs before undertaking them. If the quilt is lightly quilted, do the same in the border. If there are lots of quilted motifs and surrounding stippling in the interior areas, then feel free to stipple heavily in the borders.

*Tip*

If your quilt edges do ripple, block them flat. Moisten the edges and pat them down to dry flat.

FREE-MOTION STIPPLE QUILTING

# Machine-Quilted
## *Feathers*

F eathers are among the most beautiful quilting motifs. Elegant and flowing, they showcase the skill of the quiltmaker and add to the dimensional texture of the quilt. They also beautifully enhance the simplest patchwork. Although feathers may look difficult, with practice they are simple to stitch using free-motion machine quilting. With just a few easy steps you'll be ready to embellish your quilts with these breathtaking designs.

## Getting Ready

Set up your machine for free-motion quilting and practice your skills prior to attempting feather designs. It's important that you feel comfortable moving the fabric in any direction and following the lines of a design.

Transfer the feather motif to the quilt top or a practice quilt sandwich using an easy-to-see fabric marker. You may find it easier to start with larger feathers since the curves will be gentler, but the skills for stitching feathers are basically the same for any size feathers.

 *Refer to "Free-Motion Quilting Basics" on page 82 for pointers on practicing this type of stitching.*

*Refer to "Free-Motion Quilting Basics" on page 82 for pointers on practicing this type of stitching.*

### What You'll Need

**Sewing machine**

**Darning foot**

**Layered and basted quilt top or practice quilt sandwich**

**Thread to match the quilt sandwich**

**Feather motif pattern or stencil, 6" or larger**

**Easy-to-see fabric marker**

**Thread snips or embroidery scissors**

**Twin needle, size 3.0 or 4.0 (optional)**

## Quilting Feathers

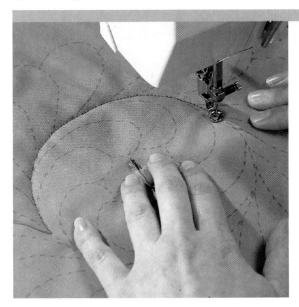

**Begin stitching the motif with the vein that runs through the center of the feathers.** This central design line is the most evident and must be smooth and well-shaped. Beginning with the vein ensures best results.

If your needle strays off of the marked vein, stop and restitch to correct the problem. See "The Quilter's Problem Solver" on page 87 for details on fixing this type of stitching glitch.

MACHINE-QUILTED FEATHERS

**2**

Feather motifs have many vein variations. The single vein in the previous step is the easiest to stitch using free-motion quilting. Multiple-lined veins require accurate stitching to ensure uniform width. **On long or large feathered motifs, like undulating borders, stitch the veins using a walking foot. For perfect width veins, use a wide (3.0 or 4.0 mm) twin needle.** The stitching appears as two straight stitching lines on the quilt front and a zigzag line on the quilt back.

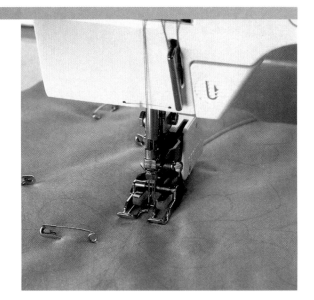

**3**

**From your stopping point, stitch to the base of the nearest feather.** You may need to stitch over some previous stitches. Take care to stitch as close to the original stitches as possible. You are ready to begin stitching the feather portion of the motif.

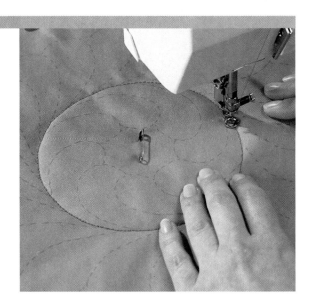

**4**

**Tip**

Remember to keep your eye on the "road"—or quilt; not on the needle. It's easier to follow the design.

Start stitching at the bottom of the feather. Stitch toward the outer curve of the feather. The actual design line may be obscured by the presser foot. **The best method for following a hidden design line is to look at the visible lines around the foot.** Most designs are very symmetrical, with all the feathers the same width and height. Judge the current stitching line by the surrounding portions of the design.

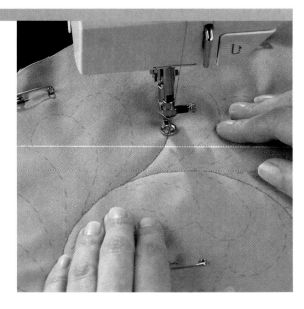

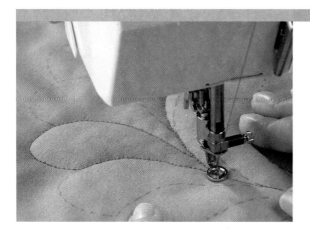

**Stitch around the outer curve and down the next line.** Stop with needle lowered into the fabric at the bottom of the first loop. You have completed the first feather. The bottom of the feather is the natural place to relocate your hands or adjust the quilt so you're ready to move to the next feather. Adjustments at this spot are the least conspicuous.

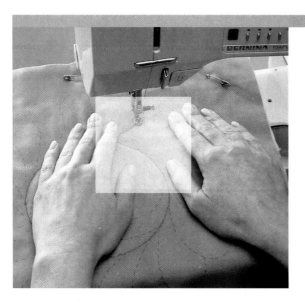

**On large motifs like feathers it's important to frequently relocate your hands or adjust the quilt. You can accurately stitch only small areas of the quilt without stopping.** For beginners, the stitching area, called the "comfort zone," may be as small as a 3-inch square. The most accurate stitch placement is in the center of the zone. As you approach the edges of the zone you begin losing control of the stitches. You have exceeded your zone when you can no longer control the quilt or move easily in any direction.

*Tip*

Use a light hold on the fabric; pressing down too heavily on the quilt prevents it from moving easily.

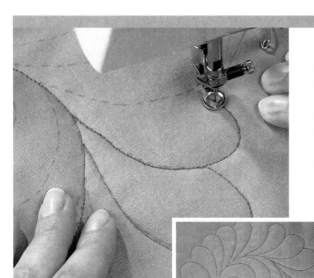

After adjusting your hands, continue stitching the feathers. **To begin a second feather, stitch over the previous line of stitching. The duplicated lines don't have to be exact stitch for stitch, but should be close.** Most traditional feather designs require duplicate stitching. Continue quilting the motif, ending where you started.

After all feathers are stitched on one side of the vein, move to the other side of the vein and stitch those feathers. For a single vein, you can simply keep stitching. For a double vein, anchor the stitches and move the quilt so the needle is in position on the second vein line, then stitch feathers in the same manner.

MACHINE-QUILTED FEATHERS

**8**

Think of feathers as simply a stylized capital letter M. Like the letter, feathers are stitched in one long smooth line. The vertical bars between the sections are double stitched. **Stitching feathers like you would write the letter *M* gives an easy even rhythm to the work.**

**Tip**

Remember to blink and breathe. Frequently beginners concentrate so intently on the design line they hold their breath or stare at the work.

 **9**

With a little planning, most feather motifs with a single vein are stitched in one unbroken line of stitching. **Beginning with the vein, start stitching at the base of a feather. Stitch around the vein, and join the end stitches to the beginning stitches.** Do not cut the thread or remove the quilt from under the machine.

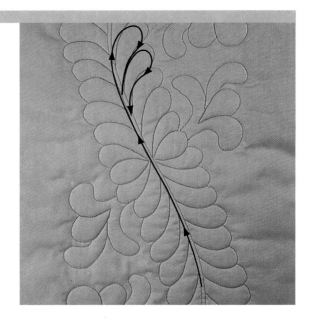

**10**

All feathers have a right or left orientation. Determine the stitching sequence for the feathers by looking at the individual feathers. **Work the right-hand feathers clockwise, or left to right. Work the left-hand feathers counterclockwise, or right to left.** It's easiest for right-handed people to stitch from left to right, just as they write, while left-handed people stitch more easily from right to left.

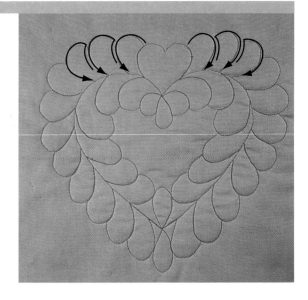

## Jagged Stitches & Uneven Feathers

| Problem | Solution |
|---|---|
| **Stitches are jagged when starting out.** | Stopping and starting while stitching often results in jagged stitching. These "hiccups" occur during the first one or two stitches of a quilting line and look like a sharp V of stitches, or a zigzag. The problem is not related to your skill in following a design line, but rather by a small, sudden movement of your hands before the machine is running. Make a conscious effort to start the machine stitching *before* moving your hands. Take one or two stitches in place, then resume quilting. |
| **Not all feathers look alike.** | This is quite common, as most quilters feel more comfortable stitching feathers in one direction rather than the other. Just remember, in nature no feathers are identical, either! If you find it hard to stitch feathers to the left of the vein, practice them a bit more until that curving action feels almost as comfortable as stitching feathers to the right of it. |

### Skill Builder

**Singing or listening to music can increase your enjoyment of quilting and improve your stitching.**

Music has many positive effects. It helps alleviate mental and physical tension by breaking the cycle of concentration and overcompensation. Intense concentration on developing quilting skills often has the negative effect of aggravating the quilter without improving her skills. Relaxation is the key to developing excellent stitch control. Music helps you to relax and develop a smooth rhythm that results in better stitch placement and size.

### Try This!

**It's best to stitch as much of the quilt as possible with the least amount of starts and stops.** An easy way to do that is to use the background filler as connection lines between motifs. Upon completing a motif, stitch along a filler line, like a grid line, to the next motif. Another excellent way to move from motif to motif is to stipple a single line between the two motifs. The single stipple line is incorporated into the overall stippling without showing.

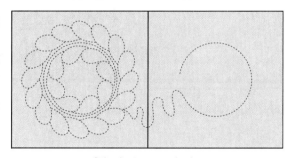

Stipple to next design

# Free-Motion
## *Echo Quilting*

**B**asically, echo quilting does just what it says—it echoes, or repeats, a shape with concentric lines of quilting. Echo quilting is a form of stippling, so it's perfect for setting off areas of a quilt you want to highlight. Since the design is repeated multiple times, use this form of quilting to emphasize a lovely appliqué shape or design element.

## Getting Ready

Echo quilting is a form of free-motion quilting, so you will use your sewing machine with the feed dogs lowered. A darning foot works best when echo quilting, and it's easiest if you layer your quilt using a low-loft batting. Use machine embroidery thread or a good-quality cotton thread in both your needle and bobbin.

You should already have appliquéd or machine quilted the motifs around which you will be echo quilting. Pin baste any areas that are not quilted, but make sure to leave enough room for the first few rounds of echo quilting. You don't want to have to stop and remove pins in the middle of a round.

## What You'll Need

**Sewing machine**

**Darning foot**

**Walking foot (optional)**

**Machine embroidery thread**

**Layered and basted quilt top or practice quilt sandwich; must have appliquéd or quilted motif**

**Nickel-plated safety pins, *or* quilt basting gun**

**Thread snips or embroidery scissors**

## Echo Quilting

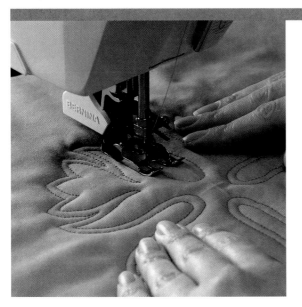

You can echo quilt around appliqué shapes or quilted motifs. In either case, the first row of echoing is to outline quilt the shape. If you're comfortable enough, you can free-motion quilt the outline. **Otherwise, temporarily use a walking foot, and stitch ⅛ inch or less from the outside the edge of your appliqué or quilted design.**

*Tip*

If echo quilting is new to you, practice by drawing your quilting scheme on paper.

FREE-MOTION ECHO QUILTING

**2**

Start the next row of stitching, using one of the methods in "Learning How to Start and Stop" on page 68. Stitch around the entire shape about ⅛ inch from your first row of outline quilting. End where you began and anchor the stitching, but don't clip the threads.

**Raise the presser foot and move about ⅛ inch outside the line of echo quilting you just stitched. Anchor the stitches and create the next row of echo quilting.** Continue stitching, spacing your lines of echo quilting evenly.

*Tip*

Start your echo quilting on a smooth part of the shape, not a corner or the tip of an angle.

**3**

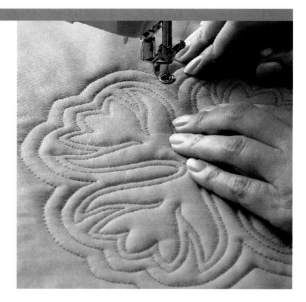

Evenly spaced rows of echo quilting is one way to go, but you can also create wonderful effects by gradually increasing the amount of space between each line of stitching. **Not only does the effect of increasing space between rows look nice, but it also helps hide any imperfections in the spacing.** Since each new row has a different amount of space before it, inconsistent spacing just becomes part of the quilting effect.

*Tip*

Don't start each new row directly next to the last starting/ stopping point, or these areas will become quite noticeable.

**4**

**Notice as you add new rows of echo quilting that the curves and indentations become less pronounced.** As you progress, each successive line of quilting will become slightly flatter than the previous one. Curves and angles will eventually become less and less defined the farther out you echo quilt.

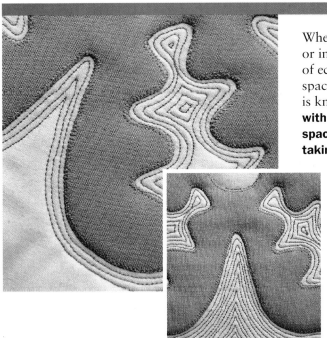

When you quilt between two shapes or inside a deep indentation, the lines of echo quilting may touch. The space formed inside where they touch is known as a pool. **Fill in the pools with concentric lines of echo quilting, spacing them ⅛ inch apart and taking care not to overlap or cross over any stitching lines.**

Just as you create pools when stitching lines merge between shapes, you'll eventually run into the edge of a block and a situation where you cannot continue a shape. **Simply quilt concentric rows that follow the shape of the converging outlines, ending each row of stitching at the seam line.**

**Tip**

Leave too large rather than too small an inside pool to avoid a blobby appearance.

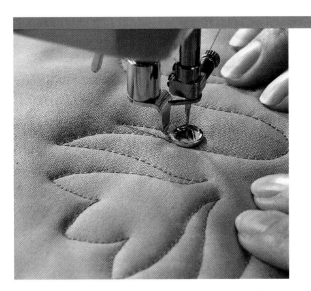

If you are having trouble getting your lines spaced evenly, try using your presser foot to judge the spacing. Some presser feet have markings, others may be wider on one side than on the other. Use these features to your advantage. Try out a few different scenarios according to your specific foot and how far apart you like your rows of stitches to be. **Here, by guiding the edge of the presser foot along the quilted design, you can ensure that the two rows are perfectly spaced.** As you progress, each row will be based on the one stitched two before it.

**Tip**

For a colorful effect, change your thread color with each round, moving from dark to light or through a rainbow of colors.

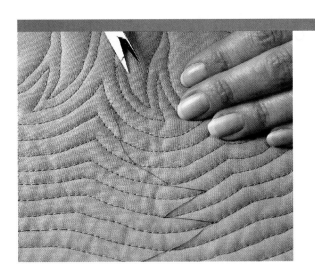

After you've echo quilted your entire background or shape, use a pair of thread snips or embroidery scissors to trim the threads from both sides of the quilt. **Be sure to clip the threads where you lifted the presser foot and moved out to begin the next round, but do so carefully!**

FREE-MOTION ECHO QUILTING

# The Basics of *Machine Trapunto*

Quilters have long had a love-hate relationship with trapunto. They love the way it looks—but hate all the time-consuming hand labor involved. Here's where machine quilting comes to the rescue. This rich-looking stuffed work becomes a totally manageable technique when you let your sewing machine do the work. Machine trapunto uses an extra layer of batting and water-soluble thread to create the same dramatic effect in much less time.

## Getting Ready

You'll need to choose your quilting design carefully for machine trapunto. To create a stuffed design, the area should be entirely enclosed, such as a flower. Designs with open lines, such as a continuous line of waves, are not suitable. See page 106 for two design ideas you can use for machine trapunto.

Choose your quilting design and mark it on your quilt top with a removable marker or silver pencil. Wind your bobbin with machine embroidery thread and thread your machine with water-soluble basting thread. (You will switch the top thread to machine embroidery thread for the quilting.) Lower your feed dogs and make sure you have a darning foot or walking foot on your machine.

Because this technique uses water-soluble thread, you will need to wet your quilt when it is finished to dissolve the thread. So, be sure your fabrics are prewashed and colorfast before beginning your project.

See page 106 for two design ideas you can use for machine trapunto.

### What You'll Need

- **Water-soluble basting thread (or .004 mm clear mono-filament thread)**
- **Water-soluble marking pen (or silver marking pencil)**
- **100% cotton machine embroidery thread**
- **Sewing machine**
- **Darning or walking foot**
- **Size 90/14 machine quilting needle**
- **Quilt top**
- **Thick polyester batting (such as "Fat Batt") or double layer of cotton batting, large enough to fill areas to be trapuntoed**
- **Nickel-plated safety pins**
- **Blunt scissors**
- **Thread snips or embroidery scissors**
- **Quilt batting, 4" larger than your quilt on all sides**
- **Backing fabric**

## Machine Trapunto

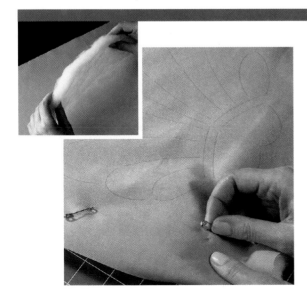

Work with your quilt top wrong side down on a flat surface. Cut a piece of thick polyester batting about 2 inches larger in each direction than your marked design. If you prefer cotton batting, use a double layer of it instead of the polyester. **Place the batting over the area you want to stuff, centering it over the marked design. Turn batting and quilt top right side up and pin securely in place.** Note: Do not add the backing fabric yet. You are only stitching the trapunto batt to the quilt top.

*Tip*

Keep pins outside the area that you'll be sewing so the presser foot can move freely around the quilting design.

**THE BASICS OF MACHINE TRAPUNTO**

## 2

**With the darning foot on the machine and the feed dogs lowered, stitch the outline of the design only, using the water-soluble thread in the machine and cotton embroidery thread in the bobbin.** When you have completed the outline, clip the threads close to the fabric. See page 84 for more information on free-motion stitching with feed dogs lowered.

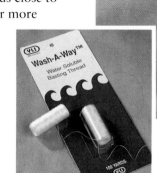

## 3

**If you prefer not to wet your finished quilt, you can substitute clear monofilament thread for the water-soluble thread.** The monofilament will remain in your quilt, though, and it may be visible when the quilt is finished. Stitch a small sample using monofilament on the scraps from your quilt to see if the results are pleasing. This is a good alternative to water-soluble thread if your fabrics are not colorfast.

## 4

**Tip**

Fiskars makes blunt scissors for children that work great for trimming batting.

When you have completed stitching all trapunto, turn the quilt over and use blunt scissors to trim away the batting outside of the design. **Cut very close to the stitches, but take care not to cut into your stitches or your quilt top.**

If you're using batting with a scrim, place the scrim side next to your quilt top before stitching. Then, after you sew, **pull the batting away from the scrim and only trim the batting, leaving the scrim in place.** The scrim will help you avoid cutting into the quilt top accidentally.

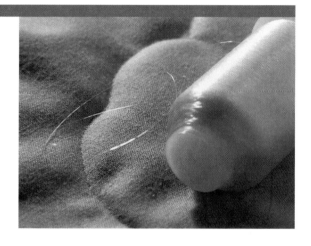

**5**

**Layer your quilt as you normally would, placing your full-size quilt batting between the wrong sides of your quilt top and backing.**

Pin baste the layers together very securely with safety pins, especially in the areas you just stuffed. The better you pin, the less likely you'll be to quilt in a pucker.

**6**

Using cotton thread in the machine and the bobbin, **quilt your entire marked design, *including repeating the outline of the design.*** Remember, if you don't stitch over the water-soluble thread, it will wash out and no stitching will be left to hold the trapunto in place.

Try to stitch directly on the previous stitches, especially if you used monofilament. If you used water-soluble thread, it's not as crucial since those first stitches will dissolve when the quilt is submerged in water. Clip the threads close to the fabric.

**7**

**To make the stuffed area even more prominent, stipple in the background around the trapuntoed area.** This will create a flatter, textured area around the raised, puffy design. See "Free-Motion Stipple Quilting" on page 88 for instructions on stippling.

*Tip*

Another type of quilting that would set off trapunto nicely is echo quilting. See page 98.

**When you have completed all quilting, immerse your quilt in clear, tepid water to remove the water-soluble thread.** Note: Do *not* add any soap or detergent to the water. Gently agitate the quilt by hand for 10 to 15 seconds.

Spread the quilt carefully on a flat surface, block it to the desired shape, and let it dry.

*Tip*

Try a hand-held steamer to steam out the water-soluble thread. (Use a marking method that doesn't have to be washed out.)

**Design Ideas for Machine Trapunto**

THE BASICS OF MACHINE TRAPUNTO

# The Quilter's
# Problem Solver

## Repairing Accidental Snips

| Problem | Solution |
|---|---|
| **Small snip in the fabric next to the stitches.** | Fuse a piece of knit interfacing to the wrong side of the quilt top, making sure to close the cut completely. |
| **Medium-size gash in the fabric.** | Fuse as above, and stipple generously over the area to disguise it and keep it closed. |
| **Hole cut out of the fabric.** | Fuse with interfacing as above, then also fuse a piece of the quilt top fabric on top of the hole. Take care to match the fabric pattern to disguise the mend. Stipple generously over the area. |

**Skill Builder**

**Practice and experiment to perfect your machine trapunto skills.**

❏ If you don't have much experience free-motion quilting, practice stitching designs on a sample quilt sandwich without fat batting. Try to stay as close to the marked design lines as possible, because once you fill the area with extra batting, straying from the line will become a little more noticeable.

❏ Stitch around the same practice design two or even three times before moving on to your real quilt to get a feel for duplicating your original stitching line.

❏ Test your trapunto design in a sample first to be sure you like it. If there's too much stuffing, you can always use a thinner batt or you can trapunto selected areas and leave others flat for contrast.

## Try This!

**Lighten the load on big projects.** When working on a project that has several (or many) areas to trapunto, don't use one large sheet of thick batting to do all the trapunto at once. Your quilt will become heavy and unwieldy, and your neck, shoulders, and arms will fatigue quickly.

Instead, cut smaller pieces off the thick batting that are just large enough to stuff one area of the quilt at a time. After stitching batting in one motif, trim the excess batting before moving to the next motif. If your quilt has many areas to trapunto, it will eventually get heavy, but you won't have to maneuver the bulk of a heavy quilt throughout the entire project.

# Twin-Needle
## *Corded Trapunto*

L like stuffed work, corded trapunto gives an elegant, rich feel to quilted projects. Unlike cording by hand, you don't need to poke holes in the back of your work to insert yarn to add a raised look to graceful vines, feathers, or other motifs. With Julia Zgliniec's innovative method for doing corded trapunto on the sewing machine, all you need is a twin needle and some cording. The machine does the stuffing and the result is a quilt that is just as beautiful on the front as on the back, or a garment that is completely reversible.

## Getting Ready

Cording traditionally is done on wholecloth projects or in plain alternate blocks in pieced or appliquéd quilts. Choose a quilting design suitable to the area you want to fill and mark it on your quilt top with a silver pencil or water-soluble marking pen. Designs that aren't too complex or don't have too many points where they cross over themselves are easiest to start with, however feathers and intricate continuous-line designs look great when corded.

Use machine embroidery thread on the bobbin, and thread your machine with .004 monofilament thread. You will switch the top thread to machine embroidery thread for the final quilting, so the monofilament will be covered. Another option is to use water-soluble basting thread from YLI for the top thread, which will entirely disappear when you wash your project. Be sure your fabrics are prewashed and colorfast before beginning your project if this is your plan.

## What You'll Need

**Quilting design or stencil**

**Zigzag sewing machine**

**Cording: cotton cording, cotton yarn, #5 pearl cotton**

**Twin needle, size 4.0**

**Silver marking pencil or water-soluble marking pen**

**Quilt top or practice fabric**

**Nickel-plated safety pins or quilt tacks**

**Water-soluble basting thread _or_ .004 mm monofilament thread**

**Walking foot**

**Blunt scissors**

**Quilt batting**

**Backing fabric**

**Size 90/14 machine quilting needle**

**100% cotton thread**

**Embroidery scissors or thread snips**

**Darning foot**

## Corded Trapunto

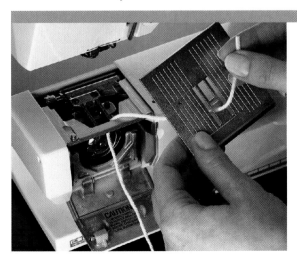

**1**

Remove the regular needle and the presser foot from the machine. **Feed the cording through the bobbin case opening and then through the small hole in the throat plate.** Leave the bobbin door open so it doesn't pinch the cording as you sew.

Once the cording is situated, insert the twin needle. A size 4.0 works well since the cording should fit between the needles without being pierced by them. The fit shouldn't be too loose, or the cording won't be emphasized.

_Tip_

Wrap the end of your cording with a bit of transparent tape and it will be much easier to thread through that tiny hole.

TWIN-NEEDLE CORDED TRAPUNTO

**2**

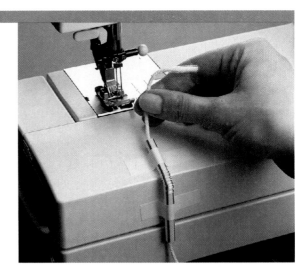

*Tip*

To make stitching easier, flatten the straw a bit so it doesn't stand up so high and cause drag on your fabric.

If your machine doesn't have a hole in the throat plate for feeding cording (it won't if you have a top-loading bobbin), you can manually feed the cording, but this can be a bit tricky.

**Instead, install your own cording feed system by taping the end of a bendable drinking straw to the front of your machine.** Feed the cording through the straw and under your presser foot.

**3**

Mark your design on your fabric with the silver making pencil or water-soluble marking pen. If you have used a stencil rather than tracing a printed pattern, you'll have gaps in the markings where the stencil bridges were. **Fill in any gaps so you'll know exactly where to sew every step of the way.** If there are gaps at the corners, it will be hard to be consistent when guiding a twin needle exactly into the corner. When marking is complete, pin baste a piece of batting under the design area.

**4**

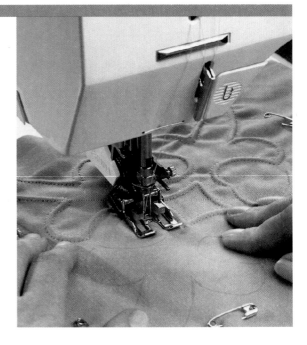

*Tip*

Don't backstitch or overlap stitching lines at the end, or cording will get too bulky.

Thread your machine with two spools of either monofilament or water-soluble thread. When you thread, make sure one thread is on one side of the tension disks and the other thread is on the opposite side. The thread in the left tension disk should be threaded through the left needle. See your machine manual for specifics on the tension disks.

**Using a walking foot, begin stitching the design. Start at a straight section, not at a curve or point.** If you are stitching an enclosed shape, the left needle should enter the fabric along the marked line and the right needle should be stitching *inside* the design area.

When you come to a point or corner in the design, you cannot simply turn the fabric with the needle lowered, as you would with a single needle. When the inner needle reaches the turn, turn the flywheel to raise the tips of the needles to just the surface level of the fabric. **Raise the presser foot, and turn the fabric halfway around the turn.** Insert the needles back in the fabric (the inner needle goes in the same hole it just came out of), lower the presser foot, and take a stitch. **Lift the presser foot, raise the needles and take another half-turn, and stitch as before to complete the turn.**

**Tip**

The stitch length from the outer needle may appear long at the turns. Don't worry—the final quilting will cover it.

**When the entire design has been stitched with the twin needle, trim away the excess batting from around the design, as you did for regular trapunto on page 104.** Use blunt scissors to avoid poking or snipping into your top fabric.

**Clip the cording edges close to the surface to prevent excess bulk in the finished quilt.**

Layer the corded quilt or project with full-size batting and backing fabric. Because it's three dimensional, the cording may make the quilt top appear to be puckered at some points and the overall dimensions will have shrunk. **Smooth it out as much as possible, then pin baste or quilt tack layers together.** The final quilting will correct this puckering.

**TWIN-NEEDLE CORDED TRAPUNTO**

**8**

Tip

If you use different threads on top and bottom, test the tension to ensure that both the front and back will look great.

Change to a machine-quilting needle, and thread it and the bobbin with cotton thread. **Using a walking foot, stitch over previous stitching. To start, pull up the bobbin thread and leave long enough tails for threading back into your quilt.** Don't take small stitches or knot threads.

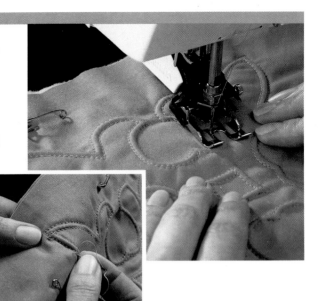

After stitching completely along one side of the cording, repeat for the other side. Try to stitch directly on the previous stitches, especially if you used mono-filament. If you used water-soluble thread, those first stitches will dissolve when the quilt is submerged in water.

**9**

Examine the finished design to see if any threads still appear, especially at points or corner areas where you pivoted. **Snip them away with embroidery scissors or thread snips.** If you used water-soluble thread, these stitches will simply wash away. **Then use a darning foot and stipple in the background around the corded area to make the stuffed area even more prominent.** See page 88 for details on stipple quilting.

**10**

**When quilting is complete, your design should look identical on both sides of the quilt.** The only noticeable difference in the sample is that the right side still has markings left in. After washing, it will be a completely reversible project with no holes poked in it. Notice, also, that the puckering that occurred after cording has disappeared now that the final quilting is complete.

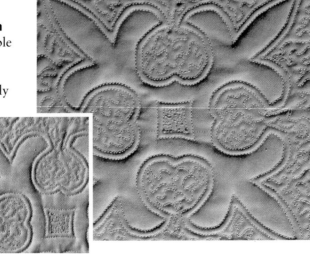

## Monofilament Thread

| Problem | Solution |
|---------|----------|
| **Monofilament snags in machine.** | Be sure to choose a reliable brand, such as YLI or Sulky. Then, before stitching on the project, test tension between monofilament and your bobbin thread. Monofilament is so fine that you may need to increase your needle thread tension. If it continues to be a problem, switch to water-soluble thread. |
| **Don't want monofilament in quilt, but don't plan to launder a new quilt either.** | If you're averse to monofilament, use water-soluble thread even if you don't plan to wash your quilt. It, too, is very fine and will easily be covered by your quilting thread, especially if you use 40-weight thread instead of embroidery-weight thread. Any bits of thread that aren't covered can simply be clipped out, just as with monofilament. |
| **Not sure which color monofilament to use.** | Monofilament comes in clear and smoke. Use clear for any light colors and smoke for dark colors. Since it will be covered with cotton thread, clear is suitable for most medium colors, too. |

**Get professional results with these tips.**

❏ Snip away stray monofilament stitches. If left in, they'll catch and reflect light.

❏ If points or corners are blunted where you turned with twin needle, be sure to "fix" them when stitching with cotton thread. Follow the marked line of the point rather than the blunt first stitching.

❏ If you prewash your fabric and preshrink your cotton batting, then preshrink your cotton cording or yarn, too. You don't want it to be the only thing to shrink the first time you launder your project!

## Try This!

**Don't reserve corded trapunto just for designs marked with stencils or printed quilting designs.** You can enhance appliqué shapes by outlining them with cording rather than a row of simple outline quilting or echo quilting. As an added bonus, the back side of your quilt will have the impact of the design shape even though it's not appliquéd.

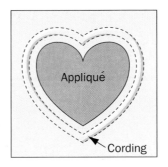

# From Basic Bar Tacks
## *to Charm Tacks*

The hand-tied, folk art style of finishing a quilt has become quite popular because it's quick, simple, and decorative. Did you realize that you can also tie your quilt by machine? Use tying—usually called tacking when done by machine—alone or in combination with other quilting techniques, as an accent, or as the main method of anchoring the quilt layers together. The methods included here range from the very simple bar tack to more elaborate and whimsical charm tacks. You're sure to find one that you like!

# Getting Ready

Practice each type of tack before you commit to using one on your quilt. Then study your quilt carefully and decide exactly where to place, how to orient, and how large or small to make your tacks. You'll want to mark each tack position on your quilt. If you're using a combination of tack types, mark which type you'll use and its orientation in each spot you want to tack.

Make sure your machine is in good working order and you have a full bobbin—there's nothing so frustrating as running out of bobbin thread in the middle of a tack. Raise the feed dogs and test your zigzag before you begin, and make sure you have a good feel for the stitch width. You'll be adjusting the stitch width while you sew, so you'll want to practice that first, as well.

# Tacking

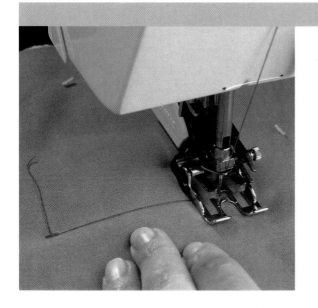

## Basic Bar Tacks

Attach your walking foot to your machine. Anchor your stitches (see page 68). Set the stitch width to its widest setting and stitch length to slightly longer than 0. **Take eight to ten stitches, stop with the needle down, then anchor your stitches again.** Raise the needle and slide the quilt under the needle to the next place you want to tack, and repeat. When you have completed all your tacks, clip the threads close to the surface of the quilt.

Enhance basic bar tacks by tacking over the center of 6" lengths of ¼" or ⅛" wide ribbons. When tacks are complete, tie ribbons into bows.

## Arrows

Anchor your stitches. Set the stitch width to 0 and the stitch length to slightly longer than 0. **As you stitch, gradually increase the width of your stitches, forming an arrow.** For a long, narrow arrow, change the stitch width more slowly. For a shorter, fatter arrow, change the stitch width more quickly.

## Diamond

Anchor your stitches. Set the stitch width to 0 and stitch length to slightly longer than 0. As you stitch, gradually increase the width of your stitches, forming half the diamond. **To complete the diamond, gradually decrease the stitch width, making sure to do so at the same rate as you increased it for the first half of the diamond.**

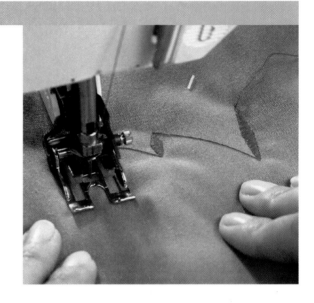

## Decorative Stitches

If your sewing machine has decorative stitches, you may want to experiment with them to see if any are suitable for tacking your quilt. **Anchor your stitches, then select the desired stitch (we used a star stitch), and make one complete design.** Change your settings back to a straight stitch with a stitch length of 0 and anchor stitches again. Raise the needle out of the fabric, move to next area to be tacked, and repeat.

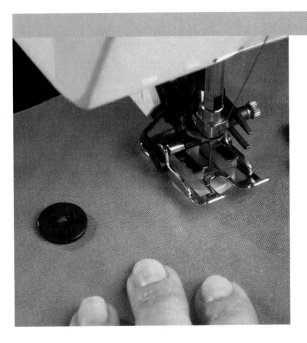

Buttons embellish as well as tack a quilt. To machine-tack a button, position it on the quilt. Turning the flywheel by hand, guide the needle into the left buttonhole. Then lower the presser foot. (Use an open-toe embroidery foot or walking foot, or any foot that can accommodate the width of the zigzag.)

Set the stitch width and length at 0 and anchor the stitches. Stop with the needle up. **Adjust the stitch width so the needle will fall directly into the right buttonhole when you sew.** Carefully sew four to six zigzag stitches to secure the button. Set stitch width at 0, and anchor the stitches.

**Tip**

To hold a button in place for stitching, dab a glue stick on its underside and stick it onto the quilt top.

## Charm Tacks

Charm tacks are small, decorative shapes that you draw or trace onto tissue paper and then stitch free-motion through all the layers of your quilt. Choose a design that can be sewn with one continuous motion (see page 58). Trace the design onto tissue paper, and pin the paper to your quilt.

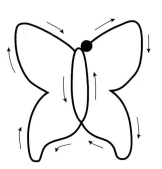

Lower the feed dogs, anchor your stitches, **then continuously stitch the design, following the lines you have drawn.** Anchor stitches again and clip the threads, leaving 3-inch tails. **Tear away the tissue paper carefully, remove any remaining pieces with tweezers,** and use a hand-sewing needle to bury the tails of thread in the batting layer of your quilt.

**Tip**

Look through children's books for small illustrations to inspire your own designs for charm tacks, or trace those shown here.

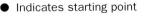

● Indicates starting point

# Machine-Quilting Secrets
## *from the Pros*

N o matter how long you've been machine quilting, it's always nice to pick up some
new tricks, especially when they come from the experts. You'll find lots of great
secrets to success in this chapter—insider tips from nationally recognized
machine-quilting teachers and award winners. Here's the place where you'll find real-life
solutions to sticky situations like how to keep the quilt taut or what to do when the bobbin
runs out halfway around a motif. You're sure to find something new you can use!

# Secrets from the Pros

## Practice on Prints

Ann Colvin recommends this easy method for practicing free-motion quilting. **Quilt on a large-scale floral print or a fabric that has oversize, simple motifs, such as fish, birds, or other animals.** Put a darning foot on your sewing machine, use a variegated thread for visual interest, and outline the shapes in the fabric. Fill them in with wavy lines, points, circles, or anything you like. You'll be learning to guide fabric through your sewing machine evenly, get a consistent stitch length, and create interesting visual texture all at the same time.

Put a border and binding around your quilted fabric and make it a wallhanging after you're finished!

## Quilt with an Embroidery Hoop

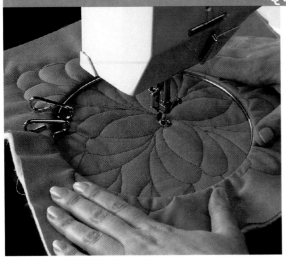

**If you have trouble keeping your quilt smooth and end up stitching puckers in the backing, use Jeannie Sexton's trick—a plastic embroidery hoop with a metal inner spring.** Place the quilt under the presser foot with the needle up, then slip the plastic outer ring under the quilt. Center it around the needle. Place the metal inner spring on top of the quilt sandwich, snapping it firmly into the plastic ring to hold the quilt smooth and taut. When quilting is complete, release the metal spring and slide both parts of the hoop to your next stitching area.

The hoop will keep the fabric from dragging on the machine bed and provides you with a handle to grip as you move the quilt.

## Stitch Points in Place

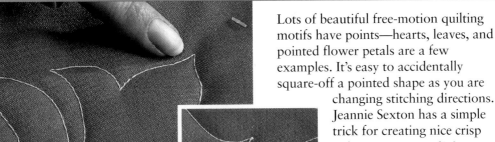

Lots of beautiful free-motion quilting motifs have points—hearts, leaves, and pointed flower petals are a few examples. It's easy to accidentally square-off a pointed shape as you are changing stitching directions. Jeannie Sexton has a simple trick for creating nice crisp points. **Take two stitches right on top of each other at the point, then continue stitching your motif.** The points will be perfect.

## Swing Your Machine Away

To maximize the amount of space on either side of your sewing machine needle when free-motion quilting, **try turning your machine 90 degrees *away from you* like Debra Wagner does, so that the head of the machine (the needle end) is away and the motor end is toward you.** You may have to stretch a bit (so take frequent breaks), but it will be much easier to manipulate a quilt and guide the fabric on both sides of the needle as you quilt.

## Hide Unplanned Stops

There's nothing as frustrating as running out of bobbin thread while quilting. But Caryl Bryer-Fallert's trick will leave you with a smooth, unbroken stitching line.

When the bobbin runs out while free-motion quilting, pull the tail of bobbin thread to the top and clip both threads close to the fabric. Insert a filled bobbin and lower the needle at a point three or four stitches before your stitching line ended. **Take several tiny stitches directly over your previous stitching, actually piercing the previous threads as you stitch.** Return to normal stitch length and clip the top and bobbin thread tails close to the fabric.

## Use Threads for Emphasis

**Tip**

For filler or background stitching, such as stippling or meander quilting, it's better to match quilting thread to the fabric so these areas blend into the background.

**Take a color cue from Anne Colvin and quilt motif outlines with thread that is slightly mismatched with the fabric.** For instance, use navy thread on black fabric, dark fuchsia on red fabric (as shown here), or white thread on muslin. The color differences make quilting motifs subtly more noticeable.

**Or give quilting some visual punch with two threads in the same needle, as Libby Leman does.** You can combine different color threads, too, for blended effects. Or combine a rayon with a cotton, or a variegated with a solid.

## Get a Grip

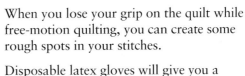

When you lose your grip on the quilt while free-motion quilting, you can create some rough spots in your stitches.

Disposable latex gloves will give you a better grip, and you can even pick up straight pins or rethread the machine while wearing them. However, your hands may get hot and sweaty. Cotton garden gloves with rubber dots on the palms and fingertips are a cooler option. **Rubber fingers from an office supply store help grip, but need to be removed to handle pins. Or, instead of wearing something on your hands, give the Quilt Sew Easy gadget a whirl.** Its foam rubber pads grip the quilt while you steer with the handles.

## Audition Designs before Stitching

Try Susan Stein's creative way to enlarge and audition quilting designs with an overhead projector. **Draw different quilting designs on paper and project them onto the quilt top, which has been pinned to the design wall.** Once you've decided on a design, the lines can be sketched onto the quilt top with a chalk pencil (do not attempt to mark with more permanent lead pencil when light conditions are not optimal). Or replace the quilt top on the wall with vellum paper and transfer the lines to that.

**Tip**

Overhead projectors aren't a typical home appliance, but check into borrowing one from work, school, church, or the public library.

## Tack without Shifting

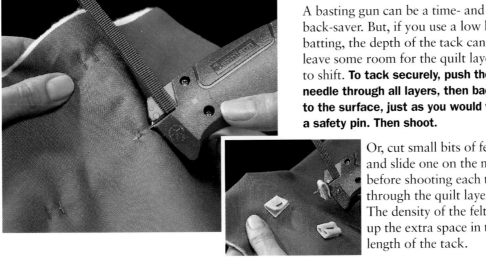

A basting gun can be a time- and back-saver. But, if you use a low loft batting, the depth of the tack can leave some room for the quilt layers to shift. **To tack securely, push the needle through all layers, then back up to the surface, just as you would with a safety pin. Then shoot.**

Or, cut small bits of felt and slide one on the needle before shooting each tack through the quilt layers. The density of the felt eats up the extra space in the length of the tack.

# Machine-Quilting Glossary

## A

**Alternative spool pin.** A free-standing apparatus or adapter that allows you to use a wider variety of threads than would normally feed properly from the machine's spool pin, including those wound on large thread cones.

## B

**Basting.** Securing all layers of the quilt so they won't shift during the quilting process. Basting can be done by hand sewing with white thread, with safety pins, or with a quilt tacking gun. See also, *Basting gun* and *Pin basting*.

**Basting gun.** A device similar to those used to apply price tags at retail stores. The gun's needle guides plastic tacks through the quilt sandwich, where they keep layers from shifting.

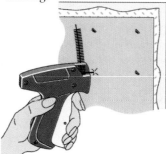

**Batting.** The "invisible" layer in a quilt. Usually made of cotton, polyester, or wool, batting is available in a variety of thicknesses. The fiber content of the batting dictates how close or far apart the quilt can be quilted to retain its shape, as well as how the finished quilt needs to be laundered.

**Bearding.** A fuzzy or "bearded" appearance that occurs when batting fibers work their way through the quilt top or backing. This condition happens primarily with polyester battings.

## C

**Canned air.** Pressurized air in a can. A quick burst removes lint from surfaces and hard-to-reach places, such as in the bobbin mechanism of your sewing machine.

**Continuous-line design.** A quilting design that can be stitched in one long, unbroken line. Helpful for machine quilting, because it eliminates stops and starts, which require you to secure thread ends. In a design such as this, the dot marks the starting and stopping point, while the arrows indicate stitching direction.

**Corded trapunto.** Stuffed quilting that is done in channels with yarn or other cording, as opposed to regular trapunto, where larger areas are stuffed with batting.

**Cording.** The string or yarn used to stuff lines of trapunto designs. Different diameters of cording can be used to create different looks. Cording options include pearl cotton, yarn, and cotton cording.

**Cross-hatching.** A grid of parallel quilting lines that form diamonds or squares. Cross-hatching can be done diagonally or on the straight of grain.

## D

**Darning foot.** A presser foot with a large opening at its base. Used during free-motion quilting, this foot moves up and down with the needle, holding fabric in place when the needle is down, but allowing free motion of the piece when the needle is in the up position.

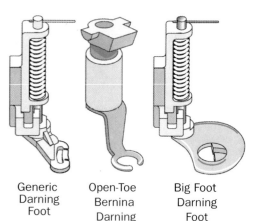

Generic Darning Foot

Open-Toe Bernina Darning Foot

Big Foot Darning Foot

**Double needle.** See *Twin needle.*

**Dual-feed mechanism.** Pfaff machines have a built-in feature that can be used in conjunction with a regular presser foot to feed top and bottom fabric layers through the machine evenly. This system eliminates the need for a walking foot attachment.

 **E**

**Echo quilting.** Concentric lines of quilting that produce repeating, or echoed, shapes. Echo quilting is most often used around appliqué shapes and quilted motifs. Rows of echo quilting can be spaced equally or by varying amounts.

**Extension table.** A work surface that fits flush with the throat plate of the sewing machine to support the quilt at one level and give you freedom to manipulate your quilt.

**F**

**Feed dogs.** A notched mechanism in the throat plate of a sewing machine that moves up and back the same length as each stitch, gripping the bottom layer of fabric to move it through the machine.

**Flexicurve.** A length of bendable plastic that allows you to mark smooth curves in virtually any shape you want.

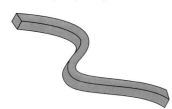

**Free-motion quilting.** Sewing with the machine's feed dogs

disengaged allows you to freely move the quilt under the needle, making stitches of any length and in any direction you choose. This type of quilting requires the use of a darning foot, which has a spring mechanism that allows it to bounce up and down on the fabric as the needle raises and lowers.

 **G**

**Grapefruit spoon.** This specialty spoon has notches at the tip to make scooping out a grapefruit section easier. They also make it easy to grip and close safety pins, which helps you avoid sore fingers when pin basting a large quilt.

 **H**

**Hera.** A traditional Japanese marking tool that leaves a sharp crease where it is pulled across fabric. The crease is used to indicate stitching or quilting lines.

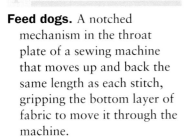

 **L**

**Latex gloves.** Disposable "rubber" gloves used by medical professionals, and anyone who wants to protect their skin while working. They are lightweight and flexible, so you can pick up pins while wearing them, yet their rubbery texture lets you grip fabric easily, so you can freely move your quilt under a darning foot while free-motion quilting.

**Light box.** A glass- or Plexiglas-topped box containing a bright light that makes tracing quilting patterns a breeze. Commercially made light boxes are available from quilt shops or art supply stores. You can make a temporary version by placing a light beneath any glass or Plexiglas table.

**Loft.** The amount of puffiness (airy thickness) in a batting. Loft can vary from very low to high or extra loft. Medium-loft batts are the most suitable for machine quilting.

 **M**

**Machine-guided quilting.** Machine quilting done with the feed dogs engaged, such as in-the-ditch, grid quilting, and gentle curves. Also referred to as straight-line quilting.

**Marking.** The process of transferring quilting designs onto the quilt top. Designs can be marked through a cut stencil with a marking pencil or traced from a printed pattern placed underneath the quilt top. Another option for machine quilting is to mark designs on paper instead of the quilt top. The paper is pinned to the quilt, stitched through on the marked lines, and torn away when stitching is completed.

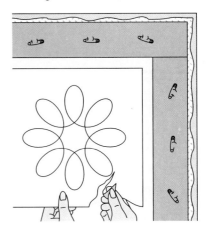

**Meander quilting.** Random quilting lines that resemble pieces of a jigsaw puzzle, and that usually don't cross over one another. When very closely spaced the lines are called stipple quilting. Meander quilting is a form of free-motion quilting.

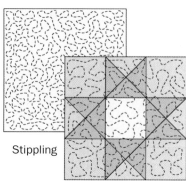

Stippling

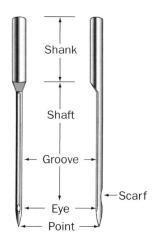

Meandering

**Milliner's needle.** A long, thin needle sometimes used to thread baste a quilt. This needle can also be used to join pieces of batting.

**Monofilament thread.** A very fine (.004 mm) nylon thread most often used through the needle only. Available in clear or smoke, the thread itself is difficult to see in the finished work. Indentations are visible, giving machine-quilted pieces a hand-quilted appearance.

**Mylar.** See-through plastic that can be used to make stencils for quilting designs. Mylar is found at quilt shops and craft supply stores. Mylar is also used to make a metallic-look "thread" which is actually flat, ribbonlike slivers of Mylar wound onto a spool. Mylar thread is available in a variety of colors.

 **N**

**Needles.** Sewing machine needles come in variety of sizes and point styles, each suited to a different need. Sizes range from a very slim 65/9 to a large 100/16. Point styles are available in quilting, topstitching, embroidery, sharp, universal, jeans, and metallic.

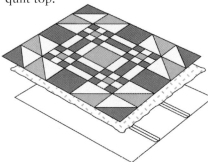

 **O**

**Outline quilting.** Quilting stitches that follow a specific design in the quilt. Outline quilting is typically stitched ¼ inch away from appliqué or patchwork shapes.

**P**

**Pin basting.** Using safety pins, rather than a needle and thread, to hold together the quilt layers.

**Point codes.** The classification system for sewing machine needles, to indicate for what use the needles are intended. For instance, H-Q stands for household machine/quilting, while H-E indicates household machine/embroidery.

**Pouncing.** A traditional way to mark a quilting motif. Holes are punched through paper along the length of the design. The paper is positioned on top of the quilt and a contrasting powder, such as cinnamon or cornstarch, is dusted through the holes to mark the design.

**Q**

**Quilt backing.** The fabric that is used for the "wrong" side of the quilt to hold the batting layer in place. Sometimes referred to as "lining." Quilt backings can be made of one piece of fabric, two or more lengths of fabric pieced together to the appropriate size, or entirely pieced to make a truly reversible quilt.

**Quilt sandwich.** The "sandwich" made by layering the backing, batting, and quilt top.

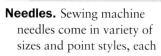

**Quilting in the ditch.** Quilting along seam lines, placing stitches very near to the seam, on the side without a seam allowance.

**Quilting thread.** Unlike hand quilting, where you need to use thread specifically made for hand quilting or wax your own thread, machine quilters have so many thread choices. Cotton, rayon, metallic, Mylar, and monofilament are the most common choices. Thread is usually selected by the look it will give the finished project, which can range from contemporary and embellished to an antique or hand-stitched look.

 **S**

**Speed bump.** A small bubble of quilt top fabric that is pushed into place as you do machine-guided quilting. The purpose is to prevent pleats and puckers in the quilt backing, a place you can't see and control as you quilt.

**Stencil.** A quilting design cut out of plastic. Quilters can draw the quilting design onto a quilt top with a quilt marking pen or pencil by marking in each slotted opening of the channel-cut stencil.

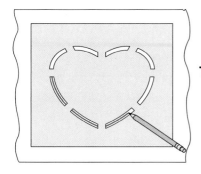

**Stipple quilting.** Very closely spaced, random lines that resemble pieces of a jigsaw puzzle, generally used to fill in small areas or flatten portions of a quilt in order to emphasize nearby raised motifs. Similar to meander quilting, but stitching lines are much closer together.

**Straight-stitch throat plate.** A machine throat plate with a hole just large enough for the needle to enter during straight stitching, rather than a wide

Zigzag          Straight stitch

hole to allow zigzag stitching. It helps eliminate puckers since fabric is not likely to be pulled into the throat plate.

**Tacking.** Machine tacking is accomplished by taking several satin stitches through the quilt sandwich in one place. Zigzag or decorative stitches can also be used. Also called tying.

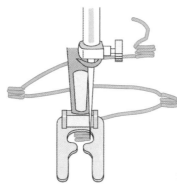

**Thread tension.** How the top and bobbin threads come together in a stitched seam. Balanced tension results in stitches that appear to be identical on each side of a sewn piece.

**Trapunto.** A method where stitched designs are stuffed with extra batting or other materials to provide a sculptured effect. See also *Corded trapunto*.

**Twin needle.** A sewing machine needle that has one shaft but two shanks and eyes so that two lines of parallel stitching can be done simultaneously. Twin needles, also called double needles, are sold by size and by how far apart the needles are. For

instance, a 2.0-80/12 needle is a size 80 and the needles will stitch 2 mm apart. Twin needles can only be used on machines that have zigzag stitch capabilities.

**Vellum.** A smooth, translucent paper that can be used to make sew-through designs for machine quilting. Sheets of baking parchment can be used in the same way.

**Walking foot.** A special presser foot that eliminates shifting and puckering by moving all layers of the quilt through the machine at exactly the same pace. Also called an even-feed foot, it is used for machine-guided quilting. See also *Dual-feed mechanism*.

**Water-soluble thread.** A thread made of spun cornstarch that dissolves when submerged in water. Often used for basting, it is also helpful for machine trapunto and corded trapunto.

**Whipstitching.** A hand-stitching technique used for (among other things) joining two pieces of batting together to achieve the size batting needed. It can also be used to join leftover pieces of batting into a larger, usable piece.

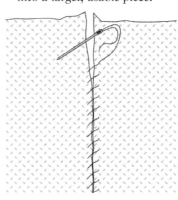

## About the Writers

**Laura Heine** has been making quilts since 1985. She is the owner of Fiberworks, a quilt shop in Billings, Montana. Laura's quilts have earned numerous awards, including the 1994 AQS Bernina Award for excellent machine workmanship. She is also a quilting teacher for YLI threads.

**Susan Stein** has been quilting since 1977. In addition to writing and designing works for publications, she teaches quiltmaking and owns a contemporary quilting store, Colorful Quilts & Textiles in St. Paul, Minnesota.

**Holice Turnbow** began quilting in the early 1970s, and since that time he has lectured and conducted workshops throughout the United States. His area of specialty is the development and use of quilting designs, and he designs quilting stencils for The Stencil Company. He is also a National Quilting Association certified quilt teacher and judge.

**Debra Wagner** is well known for her award-winning quilts. She won the Bernina Award for Machine Workmanship at the 1993 and 1995 AQS Show and Contests and her 1992 Rail through the Rockies quilt was designated as a Masterpiece Quilt by the National Quilting Association. Debra is the author of *Teach Yourself Machine Piecing and Quilting, Striplate Piecing, All Quilt Blocks Are Not Square,* and *Traditional Quilts, Today's Techniques.*

In addition, **Hari Walner** and **Jeannette Muir** graciously shared their machine-quilting techniques with us through material adapted for this book. Hari is the owner of Beautiful Publications, which publishes her continuous-line machine quilting designs, and she is the author of *Trapunto by Machine,* as well as a contributor to *Quilter's Newsletter Magazine* and *Easy Machine Quilting.* Jeannette's quilt-related experience includes teaching, judging, designing and making quilts, collecting and restoring antique quilt tops, and writing. She is the author of *Precision Patchwork for Scrap Quilts…Anytime, Anywhere,* and is a contributor to *Easy Machine Quilting* and *A Quilted Christmas.*

Thanks also to **Ann Colvin, Caryl Bryer Fallert, Libby Lehman, Jeannie Sexton,** and **Lea Wang** for their machine-quilting tips.

## Acknowledgments

We sincerely thank the many people and companies who have generously contributed to this book.

### Quiltmakers

**Stan Green,** Starlight on page 16, Town Square on page 16, and Red Star Over Cambodia on page 63.

**Nancy Johnson-Srebro,** Celebration of Cats on page 78. Quilted by Lea Wang.

**Laura Heine,** Somewhat Off Center on page 20 and Earth Day on page 102.

**Susan Nickels,** Turkey Tears on page 50.

**Ellen Pahl,** Pinwheels on Safari on page 62 and Blue and White Bricks on page 44.

*Quiltmaker* magazine, Potpourri on page 114. Designed by Theresa Eisinger; sewn by Terri Belke and Carolee Miller.

**Karen Soltys,** Amish Nine Patch on page 72 and Purple Mountains Majesty on page 10.

**Susan Stein,** Sizzle on page 32.

**Debra Wagner,** Pineapples on page 98 and blue stippled quilt on page 88.

**Joanne Winn,** Queen's Lace and Double Wedding Ring on page 58.

### Sample Makers

Many of the samples were made by the editor, Karen Soltys. Additional samples were made by Laura Heine, pages 22–24; Debra Wagner, pages 27–29 and 93–96; and Cheryl Wittmayer, pages 84–86 and 99–101.

### Fabrics and Supplies

**Beautiful Publications**—continuous-line machine quilting patterns

**Bernina of America**—sewing machine

**Dream World Enterprises**—Plexiglas extension table

**Fairfield Processing Corporation**—cotton and polyester batting

**Hobbs Bonded Fibers**—cotton, polyester, and wool batting

**Mulberry Silk & Things (a division of Hapsco)**—silk batting

**Omnigrid**—rotary-cutting mats and rulers

**Quilting Creations International**—quilting stencils

**Robert Kaufmann**—Kona Cotton fabrics

**The Stencil Company**—quilting stencils

# Index

Note: Page references in **boldface** indicate photographs. *Italic* references indicate illustrations.

# Quilting Styles

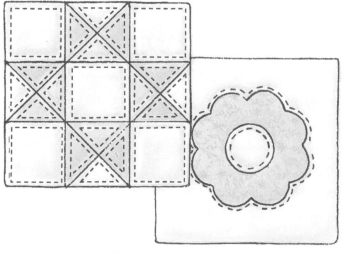

Outline Quilting

Echo Quilting

Single

Double

Crosshatch or Grid Quilting

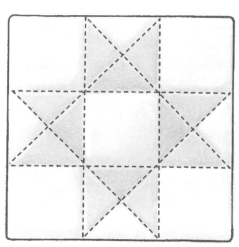

In the Ditch Quilting

Stipple Quilting

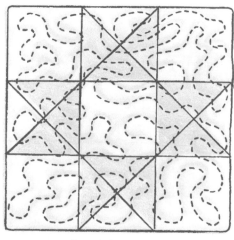

Meander Quilting